BY LILLY DANCYGER

Burn It Down:
Women Writing About Anger (editor)

Negative Space: A Memoir

First Love: Essays on Friendship

FIRST LOVE

FIRST LOVE

Essays on Friendship

LILLY DANCYGER

THE DIAL PRESS
NEW YORK

Published in the United States by The Dial Press,
an imprint of Random House,
a division of Penguin Random House LLC, New York.

THE DIAL PRESS is a registered trademark and the colophon
is a trademark of Penguin Random House LLC.

"It Comes in Waves" was originally published on
Longreads (longreads.com) in 2019. "In Search of Smoky Cafés"
was originally published in *Off Assignment*
(offassignment.com) in 2019.

Grateful acknowledgment is made to Courtney Stack for permission to include nine photographs of Lilly Dancyger to illustrate the essay "Portraiture," copyright © 2024 by Courtney Stack. All rights reserved. Used by permission.

LIBRARY OF CONGRESS CATALOGING-IN-PUBLICATION DATA

NAMES: Dancyger, Lilly, author.

TITLE: First love: essays on friendship / Lilly Dancyger.

DESCRIPTION: New York: The Dial Press, [2024]

IDENTIFIERS: LCCN 2023031368 (print) | LCCN 2023031369 (ebook) |
ISBN 9780593447574 (hardcover) | ISBN 9780593447581 (ebook)

SUBJECTS: LCSH: Female friendship. | Women—Psychology.

CLASSIFICATION: LCC BF575.F66 D35 2024 (print) |
LCC BF575.F66 (ebook) | DDC 177/.62082—dc23/eng/20230822

LC record available at https://lccn.loc.gov/2023031368

LC ebook record available at https://lccn.loc.gov/2023031369

Printed in Canada on acid-free paper

randomhousebooks.com

2 4 6 8 9 7 5 3 1

FIRST EDITION

Book design by Barbara M. Bachman

For my sisters

CONTENTS

FIRST LOVE

First Love

I sent my first love letter when I was six years old. My handwriting was blocky and large, requiring great effort and concentration to express this big emotion my little body could barely contain. I made a card shaped like a butterfly—cut out with safety scissors, decorated with elaborate colored-pencil patterns—and wrote to my five-year-old cousin Sabina that being far away from her made me feel like a butterfly with one wing.

The grown-ups called us Snow White and Rose Red, after the Grimms' fairy tale about two sisters who match their mother's two rosebushes—one that produces white roses and the other red. Though our mothers shared a sisterly resemblance, I had my Jewish father's wild curly hair and pale blue eyes, and Sabina had her Filipino father's warm brown skin and straight black hair, always brushed to a sheen and neatly braided. Dark and light, opposite twins.

"Snow White and Rose Red" (no relation to the Snow White of Disney fame, from another Grimms' story) is remarkable among fairy tales because the two sisters are not rivals or foils, but simply love each other. "The two children were so fond of one another," the story goes, "that they always held each other by the hand when they went out together, and when Snow White said: 'We will not leave each other,' Rose Red answered: 'Never so long as we live.' "

In my earliest memories, before my parents and I moved from New York to San Francisco when I was five, Sabina was always either by my side or nearby. Sometimes we lived together, and sometimes we just stayed over at each other's apartments a lot. One morning, when I was four and Sabina was three, we woke up before the grown-ups, and she said she was hungry. I could wait for my own breakfast, but I couldn't wait for hers, so I took her hand and led her to the kitchen. I pulled a chair over to the counter, where I climbed up and dug around in the cupboards until I found a salad bowl. When the adults woke up, they found us sitting on the floor, covered in milk, sharing an entire box of soggy cereal. That was always how I felt about Sabina—if she was hungry, I would climb obstacles taller than myself to bring her a whole week's worth of breakfast.

Moving three thousand miles away from her was my first heartbreak.

There's a lot of cultural mythology around the idea of a first love—that it stays with you for life, a high you never stop chasing. A magic spell cast on a fairy-tale princess, dictating the way the rest of her story will unfold.

One theory about why first love makes such an impact is that first experiences with romantic love tend to happen during our teenage years, when everything is heightened by increased hormone levels, and when the part of the brain that retains memories is maturing. This is why the music we listen to as teenagers tends to remain emotionally significant throughout our lives, and, in theory, why first teenage love stands out—a yardstick by which to measure every other love that comes after it.

But what about the first childhood experience of love, the first person you truly love other than your parents? Does a first sisterly love set the bar for a lifetime of friendships?

It's true that I've never been satisfied with friendships that stay on the surface. That my friends are my family, my truest beloveds, each relationship a world of its own. The best compliment I've ever been given was "You're so many people's best friend." Maybe I've always sought friendships predicated on deep love and knowing—been unwilling to settle for less—because I learned at such a young age that they're possible.

Sabina and I told people when we were little, "We love ourchother," and in the way adaptations of speech made by small children so often do, the phrase feels truer than the original: Between us, there was no separate "each," only "our." This was my first definition of love.

Sabina's father walked out when she was a baby and mine died when I was twelve, so as teenagers, we were both only daughters of single mothers. My mother, Heidi, was the oldest of five, and Sabina's mother, Rachel, the second oldest—the two of them bearing the deepest scars of a chaotic and traumatic childhood that included foster care, abuse, neglect, and a hippie commune. They carried the impact of their childhood instability into their own mothering in opposite ways: My mother never quite found solid ground, attempting to outrun her demons with frequent short-notice cross-country moves, and to drown them in heroin. She protected me better than her own mother had protected her, but still, I inherited chaos like a family heirloom. Rachel, meanwhile, braced so hard against the chaos that she perceived any deviation from order as a threat—like an overactive immune system reacting to something harmless, an allergy to imperfection.

When we were kids, Sabina was allergic to dairy, chocolate, cats, dogs, and at least a couple of other things. Her allergies only added to the impression that she was a delicate thing, a baby doll. The youngest cousin, the baby of the family, she even looked like a doll: big brown eyes under heavy black lashes, and perfect round cheeks. But then she'd smile—her wide, toothy grin proportionately a little too big for the rest of her face in a way that made her even more spectacularly beautiful because it reminded you that she was not a doll after all, but a real girl with a silly smile that was usually accompanied by a bubbly laugh and sometimes a little shoulder shimmy.

My mom brought me to stay with Rachel and Sabina for a few weeks the summer I was fourteen and Sabina was thirteen, when the first flashes of my teenage self-destruction were too much for her to handle. By then we'd moved back to New York, just a bus ride away from Rachel and Sabina where they'd settled in Philadelphia. My mother worked during the day and had no way to stop me from getting drunk in the park first thing in the morning and doing "god knows what else," so she dropped me off with her sister.

Resentful, I was sullen and silent the whole way to Philly. I refused to make eye contact with my mother as she ushered me out the door, onto the subway, and then onto the Chinatown bus, setting my jaw in an unmistakable pout and pulling my black hoodie over as much of my face as I could, despite the summer heat. My forehead against the window and my Converse pulled up onto the seat as the bus rolled along the New Jersey Turnpike, I blasted Nirvana's *Bleach* in my headphones and felt sorry for myself for missing out on whatever trouble my friends were getting into. I still refused to look at or speak to my mother when the bus finally stopped with a wheeze in Philadelphia, or during the cab ride to Rachel and Sabina's apartment. When my aunt opened the door to greet us, I stood with my arms crossed, scowl still on my face, making sure she, too, knew I wasn't happy to be there. I saw her and my mother exchange a glance, and prepared to dig even deeper into my sulk.

But then Sabina came bounding toward me, waving her hands in the air and yelling "Yiddy!," her nickname for me from when we were toddlers and she couldn't make an *l* sound. She was wearing a lime-green tank top with butterflies on it, so bright and bouncy and excited. She hurled herself at me, enveloping me in a big hug, completely ignoring how sour I was being. I laughed, just a little, despite myself, and returned the hug, letting her rock our bodies back and forth.

We spent those weeks being kids together—I remember them as the very last days of my childhood, which I'd been halfway out the door and away from but was willing to turn around and stay in just a little longer with Sabina. We made up dances like we used to (I picked the music—the Clash, mostly); walked around her neighborhood picking flowers; went to the library to check out big stacks of books which we read on opposite ends of the couch, our feet all in a pile together in the middle. We helped Rachel cook dinner and cleaned up together, watched movies, went to bed early and stayed up late whispering.

On one of our walks, we found a large dead dragonfly, perfectly intact, its little legs curling up in the air. We both gasped and crouched down on the sidewalk to get a closer look at its crystalline wings. "How can we get it home?" I asked, knowing we'd both already decided in our quiet awe that we would take it with us. "It's so fragile."

"Very carefully," Sabina replied with certainty, delicately picking it up by its stiff tail and laying it across her open palm. Cupping her free hand over its body to keep it from blowing away—but not touching the impossibly thin wings—she started walking again, slow and steady, with a dancer's control honed over years of ballet classes. I matched her pace, keeping my eyes on her hands and the treasure between them, and we made our way step by cautious step the few blocks back home. We spent the rest of the afternoon decorating a shoebox shrine for our new friend, agreeing that it was a sign—we weren't sure of what, but we knew it was significant.

"They were as good and happy, as busy and cheerful as ever two children in the world were," the Brothers Grimm wrote of Snow White and Rose Red.

After that summer, Sabina and I each moved deeper into our own very different worlds. We still adored each other, but as she got more serious about maintaining her perfect GPA and auditioning for school plays, I stopped going to school altogether and added cocaine to my steady diet of vodka and blunts. We had less and less common ground.

There was one time, though, the following year, when we somehow persuaded Rachel to let Sabina come with me and my friends to a punk show during a visit. I promised I wouldn't let her out of my sight, even for a second, that we'd go straight there and straight back home as soon as the show was over. When her mom acquiesced, we squeezed each other's hands and ran to get ready. My friend Haley came over—we always got ready for shows together—and we dressed Sabina up in my clothes, striped tights and a miniskirt, and mussed up her thick, sleek hair with hairspray.

When it was time to do her makeup, Sabina sat on the arm of the couch, turned her face toward me, and closed her eyes. I paused for a moment with the eye shadow palette in my hand, just looking at her, so happy she was there. I remembered all at once the way I loved her when we were little—like she was the most special person in the world, and we loved ourchother, and wasn't that just incredible? I remembered us playing dress-up, drawing circles on each other's cheeks with our mothers' lipsticks, clipping ribbons into each other's hair, dusting each other head to toe with glitter. From the smile on her face as I streaked her eyelids with black, I thought she must be remembering, too.

On our way to the show, after we'd met up with a couple more of my friends and I'd introduced her proudly to everyone, I offered Sabina a sip of vodka from my flask. I knew she wouldn't take it, but didn't want to exclude her as the rest of us passed it around. She said "No, thank you" in the same sweet voice she used when she was offered seconds at the dinner table, batting those long eyelashes. I took smaller sips than usual, remembering that I had to keep track of her and make sure she was safe and having a good time. I wanted to pull her into freedom the way she'd grounded me in ease that dragonfly summer.

As we pushed our way into the dense, sweaty crowd at the show, the dark room hot and humid and smelling of bodies and beer, the band loud enough to drown out our thoughts, I hooked my elbow into Sabina's and clasped her hand, yelling over the noise, "Don't let go!"

I was used to the pure release of the pit: hurling my body into the throng of strangers and letting it be swept up in their thrashing. My feet finding the ground only to launch back into someone's sweaty torso, someone's waiting hands, shoulders, arms; pushing each other and catching each other and not minding the sharp elbows or the heavy feet or the sudden shoves. Letting the tension be pummeled out of my body. But this time, arm in arm with Sabina, I hesitated as we approached the writhing mass. What if she got hurt? It was too late now, though; we were here. I wanted to share this with her, and she was eager, waiting for my cue.

"Ready?" I yelled over the frontman's screams, the guitar's squealing feedback, the thudding bass. She squeezed my hand and nodded, a pursed, mischievous smile on her face. I demonstrated how to hold her free arm up to protect her face; making a fist and tensing the arm so it wouldn't be jostled down. She mirrored my gesture, and in we went, holding on to each other and jumping into the churn of bodies, sweat and breath moist in the air like a greenhouse. I maneuvered us so she was closer to the periphery, the safer boundary of arms and hands ready to push her back in if she started to tumble out, my body a buffer between her and the flailing closer to the center of the pit, absorbing the kicks and elbows so they wouldn't reach her.

As we were carried around the circle by the momentum of the crowd, Sabina yelled and kicked along with everyone else, in wide-eyed delight. I saw her hair flying through the air, her face both focused and far away, and knew she was feeling it. The release.

Some psychologists believe there's an imprinting mechanism at work with our first loves—that they set the mold we'll spend the rest of our lives looking for another version of.

There has always been a protective side to my love for my friends—I will always put myself closer to the center of the mosh pit. I got into a fight once because some mean girl called my friend Sydney ugly on her birthday, so I punched her in the face. When we were teenagers hanging out on the Lower East Side, I used to walk my friend Heather home all the way to the South Street Seaport because I didn't want her walking through desolate downtown streets alone late at night—perfectly fine to make the same walk back on my own. And when a guy who'd treated Haley badly wouldn't stop calling her, I answered her phone and threatened to castrate him with my pocketknife. He stopped calling.

To love someone, I have always understood, is to keep them safe.

I spent my teenage years seeing how far I could wade out into danger before something stopped me. Fear, pain, death; any kind of limit would do. Nothing stopped me from dropping out of high school in ninth grade or drinking cheap vodka until I blacked out, so I raised the stakes. Nothing stopped me from getting into fights that left my face and knuckles bloody or going into basement apartments with strange men, so I raised the stakes again. Nothing stopped me from snorting coke in public bathrooms or staying out for days at a time. I searched and searched until the one limit I finally found was my own exhaustion—my own dwindling will to keep running toward a wall that never materialized.

Meanwhile, Sabina was raised with so much structure there was barely space for her to so much as slouch. She washed her face and hands before setting the table for dinner each evening, where she said please and thank you and then cleared the dishes without being asked. She did her homework every day promptly after school, excelled in dance and theater, and quietly bided her time until the moment she could break free.

That moment finally came when she moved out of her mother's apartment on the morning of her eighteenth birthday, to everyone's surprise. She shaved an undercut and started dating a skater boy with his own clothing line, modeling for local designers all over Philadelphia, and going to clubs to dance all night. She got really into Girl Talk and started writing and recording her own music, blooming ferociously into her own person.

That same year, I was starting college, having eked in despite a high school transcript consisting entirely of a single semester of failing grades. I was slowing down and finding some semblance of stability and routine just as Sabina was branching out and finding her freedom, and we met in the middle, a blissful reunion. I had been waiting for her to arrive, to stop being a kid. But she had probably been waiting for me, too—to stop being so angry all the time so we could be at ease in the world, together.

She came to visit, and we went to hang out with some friends of hers in Brooklyn. We sat on the floor of their sparsely furnished living room and passed around a joint. Sabina gave me a sheepish look before taking a hit, and I beamed at her—the first time I'd ever seen her do anything illegal, or even illicit.

When her friends decided they wanted White Castle, Sabina and I volunteered to go get it even though we were both vegetarians. An excuse for an adventure. Only the drive-through window was open, but they wouldn't let us order because we were on foot. "Even if we go like this?" Sabina asked, squatting to a seated position and raising her hands to an imaginary steering wheel. I followed her lead, settling into the "passenger seat" beside her. The White Castle employee wasn't amused, answering flatly, "Uh, no." We collapsed onto the asphalt, gasping with laughter, falling all over each other. The whole way back to the apartment, empty-handed, she kept yelling, "No burgers if you don't have a car!" and we'd crack up all over again.

The next day, we walked around the East Village holding hands like when we were little, talking about our respective plans for the future—she wanted to keep making music, and modeling, and thought her boyfriend might be "the one." I was loving school after so many structureless years, and thought I might want to be a professor eventually. We talked about how we hoped our future children would be close like we were; and how much it meant to us, as only children, to have someone who understood our family's particular neuroses and baggage.

When it was time for her to go home, I walked her to the bus stop—wanting to enjoy every minute of our time together, and not wanting her to have to navigate unfamiliar streets on her own. Before she got on the bus, we squeezed each other tight and both said we'd had *such* a good time; understanding that this had been more than a fun visit—it had been a return to each other.

Another theory about first love is that its lasting impression comes down to what's known as the primacy effect—a psychological principle that states that people will recall the first item on a list more reliably than subsequent ones. This applies not only to lists but to broader experiences—you remember the first time you tasted a favorite dish but not necessarily the tenth, you remember the first time you ever saw the New York City skyline from an airplane more clearly than the twentieth. You remember your first love forever.

Technically, the first people I loved were my parents. But that's a different kind of love, an imbalanced love, where the expectation is that most of the care will flow in one direction—at least early on. And it's something of a given. Not everyone has loving parents in their early life, but when you do, you don't tend to imagine it could be any other way. Your parents are there like the sun, like bedtime, like sustenance.

But the first time you love someone outside that immediate sphere of built-in love, it's a revelation. Loving Sabina was how I learned what it means to want someone else's happiness as badly as I want my own. Seeing her arrive somewhere and run toward me right away was how I learned that being loved by someone you love can be the most thrilling feeling in the world.

Sabina came to New York for my twenty-first birthday, to the party with all of my friends who were so excited to meet her.

Heather threw her arms around Sabina as soon as she walked in the door, then apologized and said, "I've just heard so much about you!" Sabina laughed and hugged her back. So many times that night I looked around the room and spotted her there, smiling at me over her red plastic cup, and was flooded with the same grateful joy I felt when I saw her at our daycare. What a gift to love and be loved so earnestly.

The following year, with Sabina's twenty-first coming up, we made plans for me to make the reverse trip to Philly to attend the big nightclub bash her friends were throwing for her, to step into her world like she had stepped into mine. "I don't think I own anything hip enough for your crew," I teased when we were talking on the phone about what we'd wear. "Don't worry," she said, laughing. "I'll make sure you look hot." I looked forward to letting her dress me up for her party, like I'd dressed her for that show years before. Like we'd been doing for as long as I could remember.

Three weeks before the party, I woke up to a missed call from my aunt Rachel. I couldn't remember her ever calling me, and had a feeling something was wrong. I thought maybe my mother was hurt or sick; her health wasn't great. I decided to make coffee and wash my face before calling Rachel back—to clear my head and brace myself. But still, when she said, "They found a body. They think Sabina is dead," the words got all jammed up on their way into my brain, so they didn't make any sense. Rachel was crying, but I latched on to the phrase "They think," certain this must be a mistake.

"But it might not be her, right?" I asked, my voice high and urgent.

"No, they think it is," she said. There it was again: They *think*.

I hung up the phone convinced that this would be cleared up. I called Sabina, the sound of my heartbeat competing with the sound of the phone ringing and ringing. Only when I heard her singsong voice on her outgoing message, "Hiii, it's Sabina," did it start to sink in.

Finally, on a delay, I heard the rest of what Rachel had said: They'd found Sabina's phone and her digital camera next to the body they "thought" was hers. The body of someone who had been murdered. As the voicemail message ended and the beep sounded in my ear, I realized that the phone I had just called was in a police station, in an evidence bag.

I can still hear the sound of myself screaming and falling to the floor. I landed on my knees with a crack that would hurt later, sobbing so hard there were little red lines of burst blood vessels around my eyes for days. On my hands and knees, I started to dry heave, my body not understanding what was happening, only that something was very wrong—as if maybe I could puke up whatever was making me feel this way.

When I wrote to Sabina of the butterfly with one wing all those years earlier, I hadn't considered the violence of that image. Hadn't pictured a hungry bird or a cruel child capturing a beautiful creature and tearing its body in half.

I remember the rest of that summer like wading through a poisonous fog. A burning in my throat, throbbing in my temples, ringing in my ears. Disoriented and nauseous. Under the haze of grief were sharp spikes of guilt: I was a hundred miles away when Sabina was killed, but I still felt like I should have been there to protect her. That was my job—to put myself between her and danger. To absorb the blows. To keep her safe.

It didn't make any sense that she was the one this happened to. All those years I spent putting myself knowingly, boldly in harm's way. I'd been getting into strangers' cars to buy drugs while she was sleeping soundly in her bed—still abiding by a set bedtime well into her teens. I'd physically threatened men twice my size on more occasions than I could count and always walked away unscathed, and she was killed steps from her front door—minding her own business and just trying to get home.

She'd just started really living her life. We'd just found our way back to each other. It didn't make any sense.

In the story of Snow White and Rose Red, much is made of the fact that the girls don't come to any harm while playing in the woods near their house, even when staying out late.

"No mishap overtook them," the story goes. "If they had stayed too late in the forest, and night came on, they laid themselves down near one another upon the moss, and slept until morning came, and their mother knew this and did not worry on their account."

This needs to be specified—it's even repeated more than once—because it goes against the usual fairy-tale trope of the woods as a dangerous place; especially for pretty young girls. "Little Red Riding Hood," a classic example, is a story used to warn girls to look out for the wolves that are waiting out there, hungry to eat them up.

But the wolves are not what interest me here. The murder. This is not a crime story, it's a love story.

With romantic love, there's usually the expectation that you get one at a time. But sisterly love allows for multiplicity, overlapping and interlocking—the first love, the one that set the bar, continuing alongside all the other loves that follow.

So if a first sisterly love is the template, does tragedy in that first formative love ripple out to all the others, like a web?

I spent most of the summer after Sabina died sitting on my fire escape in the East Village with a bottle of whiskey. I sat out there for hours at a stretch, but I remember perpetual dusk. And I remember my friends coming and going, taking turns sitting with me. My roommate, Leah, made sure I had whiskey and cigarettes and water, persuaded me to eat sometimes, and sat with me for a little while every evening before she left for work. Heather came and sat for hours and hours, even though she was afraid of heights, conspicuously avoiding looking down at the street five stories below. Haley came, driving down to the city from college upstate to sit with me and hold my hand. Carly came, and let me talk but also let me sit in silence, not giving off even a whiff of anticipation that would make me feel like I needed to say anything. Liz came, climbing in and out of the precarious window to get more ice, more booze, a light; getting just as drunk as I was until once in a while, I forgot why we were out there for a few minutes while we talked and laughed about something else.

I loved them all so much that summer, more than I ever had. I saw so clearly their love for me, how lucky I was to have them, how much each of them meant to me. I'd never been shy about telling my friends I loved them—that unselfconscious love I learned from loving Sabina—but that summer, now that I'd seen how suddenly I could lose any one of them, my love felt freshly urgent. I wanted to pull these women to me and hold them there, keep them in my sight where I knew they were safe, keep them within arm's reach where I could pat the backs of their hands and smooth their hair and tell them they were loved. To make sure each of them knew just how special she was to me, before it was too late.

Sitting on that fire escape, my legs going numb from the hard metal bars, a summer evening breeze blowing, I looked at the beloved friend to my right as she took a drag of her smoke and stared far out down the avenue, and the beloved friend to my left as she took a sip of whiskey out of her mason jar, and I remembered how I felt when Sabina was around: that I was so lucky to love someone so special, and to be loved by them in return.

Best Friends Forever

Early childhood was lemon ice and the guy on the street corner with a boombox blasting Marvin Gaye, sprinklers in Tompkins Square Park, potato pierogi, the rumble of the subway. My cousin Sabina and I walking hand in hand through the vast, enchanted land of industrial Bushwick; the watercolor of cityscape, of family all around and my best friend by my side. This was the idyll I spent years straining to return to after my parents and I left New York right before I started kindergarten.

In San Francisco, my two best friends were a pair of sisters—one a few months older than me and the other a year younger. I slipped right in as a middle sister, playing board games and learning not to put my elbows on the table. My parents were splitting up, the cross-country move having failed to solve their problems. They were trying and failing, together and then separately, to get off of heroin. Moving, together and then separately, from one apartment to another; filling each one with the sound of screaming fights. But at Katherine and Miriam's house, the trundle bed was always ready for me, dinner always served at the same time every evening.

—

The summer before I started fourth grade, my mother moved us three hours down the California coast to live in an unsettlingly quiet small town with her new boyfriend. We moved into a big house, so much bigger than any apartment we'd had before, next door to a family with a daughter my age. The day the Spice Girls split up (I still remember the exact words the TV news anchor used: "Check your spice racks, folks . . . the Ginger's missing!"), Britney and I both ran out of our houses to tell each other the terrible news, meeting under the canopy of eucalyptus and gripping each other's arms, wide-eyed and breathless with disbelief.

My mother and the new boyfriend broke up after two years in that big house, and she and I moved back across the country, to Buffalo. Our new downstairs neighbors' apartment smelled like Steak-umms and Kools, but in Shirley's bedroom we spritzed enough watermelon body spray to drown out her mother's cooking and smoking; and the rest of the world. We watched *Never Been Kissed* and *Ten Things I Hate About You* and *Clueless* like they were instructional videos. We plucked our eyebrows into oblivion and rubbed cold cucumber-scented gel on our faces, the goo of an adolescent chrysalis, eagerly awaiting transformation.

Before Shirley and I could spread our teenage wings together, though, it was back to California and my mom's boyfriend again—this time after only a year. At least this meant I'd get to see my father more, I thought; he was living just a few hours' drive from the military-base-turned-suburb we were moving to.

But then, our boxes already packed, my father died in his sleep. Instead of the camping trip we'd planned for our reunion—redwood trees and campfires and s'mores, and little figures he could carve with his pocketknife so quickly they seemed to spring to life—a funeral.

After decorating yet another new bedroom while numb with grief, I didn't have the energy to make a new best friend all over again. I would go it alone this time, I decided. I dressed in black and practiced my sullen glare; didn't scan new classrooms for the smart girls, eyes twinkling with mischief, like I usually did.

But there was another girl at school who wore a lot of black, and soon, despite my plans, Emily and I were spending long afternoons sitting high in the tree in her front yard, hiding from the world together. We wrote messages addressed "to the freaks" and signed "—Alice and Dorothy" on scraps of paper, tied them to balloons, and watched them drift up, up, up into the California sky so blue it almost hurt to look at.

The next time my mother told me we were moving was different from all the others: This time, we were finally going home—back to hot asphalt and bustling streets and good pizza and always something to do, somewhere to go, something to see.

As soon as we arrived back in New York City, I felt vividly, chokingly alive, like breaching the surface of a pool after being held under. So alive I couldn't sit still, couldn't focus at school. I skipped class with my new friends Raiona and Rakhel, and we rolled our own cigarettes lying in the grass in the park, vibrating with freedom.

Tompkins—the same park from my childhood memories—was where the kids who would rather drink malt liquor and go to punk shows than do homework congregated. Soon I didn't have just one new best friend, but a whole crew.

We stomped up Avenue A in our combat boots, arms linked, scream-singing the Ramones. Smoking and spitting, anything but sweet and pretty. We pissed between cars late at night; barely hid our bottles of liquor between big swigs, daring anyone to say something; left the park at closing time, waited fifteen minutes, and hopped the fence to go right back to where we'd been sitting. We chased bad boyfriends and random creeps out of the park, howling threats like wild dogs.

We also held each other on our laps and dried each other's tears like mothers and babies. We passed the same five bucks back and forth, covering pizza and booze; shared packs of cigarettes. Whenever anyone got too drunk or high, we balled up a hoodie and propped it under her head, and then sat right next to her, standing guard until she was ready to get up again. We traded books—Plath and Rilke, Solanas and Lorde—wrote each other stories and letters and poems, made up songs at three in the morning. We drew each other's portraits, read each other's tarot cards, pierced each other's ears and faces with safety pins.

We snarled and bristled, puffed ourselves up and bared our

teeth—but only to protect the softness we'd made for each other, where no one else had.

When my mother again started listing other places we could live—back to California, or maybe Montana, or Canada—I told her she could move again if she wanted to, but I wasn't going anywhere.

Prison Break

We stayed up all night to meet Sydney at Port Authority. We hadn't heard from her since she was sent away—we weren't even sure exactly where to, but rumor was it was the type of place where they made kids scrub the stairs with toothbrushes as punishment, and maybe worse. And we knew for sure she wasn't allowed access to a phone, or she would've called. But then we got word, thirdhand and not entirely reliable, that she was making a break for it. So me, Heather, and Raiona killed time eating midnight falafel at Mamoun's and walking slowly from the West Village to Midtown to meet her bus at dawn.

We weren't sure she'd even be there—maybe she'd get caught, maybe she'd change her mind, maybe the message had been passed on wrong and she wasn't coming at all. But just in case, we had to be there to meet her.

As we descended the creaky escalator, we scanned the crowd of sleepy people milling around the fluorescent-lit basement, rolling suitcases behind them, stopping to look at the arrival and departure board before shuffling off to wherever they were headed. It was so early in the morning you could argue it was still night, but there was no time of day at Port Authority—just low ceilings, and numbered doors opening into the subterranean parking lot.

Then there she was: about a hundred yards away, her red hair short and recognizable. I thought of the very first time I saw Sydney, at our high school orientation two years earlier: Her hair was even shorter then, in a crew cut, and she was wearing Docs and a red tulle petticoat as a skirt. My hair was faded purple and I was wearing a Buzzcocks T-shirt. We made eye contact across the auditorium and gave each other a small chin-up nod that said, "Yes, we're going to be friends."

"There she is!" I stage-whispered to Raiona and Heather. I didn't yell or run, trying not to draw attention, but I started walking quickly toward Sydney, willing her with my mind to turn toward us, and to play it cool.

Before I could catch Sydney's eye, there were two dark blurs in my peripheral vision, sweeping in from both sides and merging into a hard dark wall right in front of me. Then I blinked and it wasn't a wall; it was two police officers, standing tall and immovable directly in my path. They appeared so swiftly I almost walked right into their polyester chests. Surprise and fear splashed across my face for a whole second before I remembered to look casual, like I had no idea what they might want with us.

Sitting in the mini police station inside Port Authority, I asked the gruff officer typing up his report with his meaty pointer fingers if I could at least see my friend. "We haven't seen her in so long," I said.

He shook his head no, without looking up.

I felt my throat tighten but refused, on principle, to cry in front of a cop. Sitting on the hard plastic chair, I dug around in my bag for anything that could be a message—for once, I didn't have a pen and paper. I tried again in a sweeter voice, twisting the rubber keychain of Sally from *The Nightmare Before Christmas* off of my apartment keys, asking, "Could you maybe give this to her?"

"It's just a keychain," I pled, keeping my voice young, holding it up to demonstrate that it wasn't a weapon or drugs or anything nefarious.

His face softened, just a little, just for a second—a flicker of compassion for these crazy kids. He held out his hand and I placed the small figure on his broad palm, saying "Thank you, thank you," even though he still hadn't spoken, hadn't agreed to anything. For all I knew, he was going to throw it away.

I knew a keychain wouldn't be much comfort to Sydney when they carted her back to that place, and they'd probably take it from her anyway. But I wasn't sure if she'd seen us in the crowd before we all got herded away to separate little rooms, and I needed her to know that we'd been there. I needed her to know that in a world that doesn't tend to believe teenage girls when they say the need to escape is urgent, we—other teenage girls—had believed her. Without any details, without even speaking to her directly, we'd heard that she'd had enough, and we'd shown up to help.

Partner in Crime

It's clear from the very beginning of *Heavenly Creatures* that the film's central love story is doomed. This didn't really register for me on my first few viewings, but it's right there in the opening moments: A shaky handheld shot of two pairs of blood-splattered legs in ankle socks, running down a wooded trail. The sound of panicked screams. When we finally see the girls' faces, emerging from the woods and stumbling onto the street, they're covered in blood.

"It's Mummy, she's terribly hurt!" one girl calls out to a bystander, a woman who's come out of her house to see what all the commotion is about.

"Please," the other gasps, "help us!"

And then the story starts in earnest: We flash back to the Christchurch Girls' School, where Pauline and Juliet first meet. We follow along as they become an inseparable pair, so enamored with each other that their love carries them away from reality—and toward the violence of that opening scene.

I was in middle school the first time I watched *Heavenly Creatures*, a few years younger than Pauline and Juliet. My mother and I had recently moved to a California suburb to live with her boyfriend, whom I hated almost as much as I hated all of my new cliquey, Hollister-wearing classmates. The best-friend bond between the two outsiders (played by Melanie Lynskey and Kate Winslet) was everything I hoped was waiting for me up ahead, in teenagerdom. The love story's violent end didn't dissuade me from idealizing it—if anything, it only made it seem even more mythic. After all, everyone knows that all the most romantic love stories are tragedies.

The 1994 Peter Jackson film is based on the true story of 1950s New Zealand teenagers Pauline Rieper and Juliet Hulme. Pauline is working class, portrayed as disheveled and sullen; Juliet, the new girl in school, is rich, poised, and impertinent, correcting a strict French teacher's grammar within moments of joining the class. At this, Pauline smiles to herself as she draws in a sketchbook instead of attending to her lesson, already smitten. I was too. As the smart-ass who highlighted unclear language in my middle school student handbook looking for loopholes in the dress code, and the loner with less money than most of my classmates, I saw myself in both girls. Watching them find each other made me ache.

The jarring opening scene isn't explained until near the very end, but it's the reason the real-life pair were immortalized, infamous enough for a movie to be made about their love four decades later: When Juliet's parents decided to send her to live with relatives in South Africa, the girls became set on Pauline going with her. There was just one problem—Pauline's mother would never let her go. Convinced that she was the only thing standing in the way of their staying together, the two girls bludgeoned Pauline's mother, Honorah, to death with a brick in a stocking in Victoria Park. An inverted *Romeo and Juliet.*

I started high school in New York shortly after another move, still feeling like an outsider, still looking for a best friend who would contextualize me; someone I could love enough that it would make me make sense. I made friends quickly at my new school, clicking immediately with Sydney, who had a short spiky haircut and perpetually smudged eyeliner and an encyclopedic knowledge of all the coolest bands and books; Rakhel, an Israeli Satanist with an endearing scratchy laugh, who wore the same pleated pinstripe miniskirt every day; and Raiona, smiley and sweet on the surface but with a spark of the absurd in her bright blue eyes, like a cross between Laura Dern and Salvador Dalí. We staked out a corner of the schoolyard where we smoked cigarettes and passed a Poland Spring bottle full of vodka around, went to shows at ABC No Rio and CBGB and Arlene's Grocery on the weekends, and spent long afternoons lying in the grass of Tompkins Square Park.

But it wasn't until after I dropped out halfway through freshman year that I met the Juliet to my Pauline. The fenced-in yard of the high school I no longer attended was at the very end of Houston Street, right across from the FDR. Beyond the highway: the river. The afternoon sun seemed to hit the far corner of the yard with heightened intensity, there at the edge of the island, like it was jutting out just a little farther from the earth. At that preternaturally sunny corner, I would sit and wait, cross-legged on the sidewalk, leaning back against the outside of the chain-link fence and looking out across the water toward Brooklyn, for my friends who were still in school to finish their day so we could go to the park. This habit infuriated the guidance counselor, my erstwhile nemesis, and I delighted in reminding her with a smile and a shrug, when she told me I couldn't be there, that I was on city property.

One day, toward the end of the school year so the air already felt like summer, Sydney was sitting on the corner when I arrived, with two friends of hers from the neighborhood who I didn't know. I sat down to join them and introduced myself, pulling a pack of Lucky Strikes out of my bag. I took one for myself and then held out the open pack, offering. One of the girls, Haley, declined and said she'd just quit.

"Me too," I said as I cupped my hand around the cigarette to shelter my lighter from the breeze coming off the river. She laughed, loud and sharp, and said, "Yeah okay, I'll take one," reaching for the pack with her long, spindly fingers; that bright sun picking up the red highlights in her dark brown curls.

It was a small interaction—a passing quip and a shared smoke. But it strikes me now that the first thing I ever said to Haley other than my own name was "Me too," a phrase that would echo back and forth between us through the rest of our friendship as we relished all the ways we were similar, and then began to reshape our personalities and preferences to become more and more alike.

Early on, Pauline and Juliet bond over their respective traumatic medical histories—both had been hospitalized as girls, Pauline for a bone marrow infection and Juliet for tuberculosis—when they're the only two sitting on the sidelines during gym class. Juliet asks to see the scar down the front of Pauline's shin, declaring "That's so impressive" and asking to touch it; eager to get close to the very parts of Pauline that she was most used to keeping hidden. This was what it felt like when Haley and

I first started spending time just the two of us, branching off from our larger network of mutual friends; when we sat on a stoop, chain-smoking as I told her how much I was still reeling from my father's death three years earlier, how my mother and I fought like rivals in an ancient feud, how my whole body hummed with anxiety when I couldn't sleep in the middle of the night; and she told me things about her life that are not mine to repeat here—like showing each other our scars.

"Cheer up," Juliet tells Pauline. "All the best people have bad chests and bone diseases. It's all frightfully romantic."

The idea that the very things that have made you feel different and wrong are not only *impressive* and *romantic*, but they can connect you with someone else, is intoxicating. Irresistible. It feels like acceptance and absolution, like being fully seen and loved for exactly who you are. It feels like finding a larger-than-life cinematic love; like everything I'd hoped for when I was stranded in California, far from home and feeling so very alone. Haley and I reflected back to each other everything we wanted to see in ourselves, each gushing about how hot and smart and funny and amazing the other was—starting to believe all of these things about ourselves in the process.

We winged our eyeliner the same way, and got pierced together so we'd match—her adding a hole in her nose and me adding one in my tongue. Once my new piercing healed, we shared a collection of tongue rings, trading them regularly in an exaggerated display of intimacy. Sometimes we mixed and matched, each wearing half of two different barbells; a fleshy, spit-covered version of those necklaces with two halves of a heart. We greeted each other by pressing our tongues together in a wet high five, metal clicking against metal.

Haley was three inches taller and brunette to my blonde, but people started to regularly mistake us for each other—the long curly hair with a little too much gel so the ends were stiff, the matching homemade miniskirts and striped tights and Doc Martens, the exact same shade of bright red lipstick, and silver rings on every finger. We created ourselves around each other, like two trees growing intertwined, and soon lost track of where one of us ended and the other began.

Pauline and Juliet escape their boring schoolgirl lives by creating an increasingly elaborate fantasy world, a rich and layered mythology about another realm they call "the Fourth World," complete with saints (based on their favorite actors and opera singers), a royal family of the imagined country of Borovnia, and the girls' own Borovnian alter egos. In *Heavenly Creatures,* Borovnia is depicted in Claymation, elevating it far beyond a mere game of make-believe. For the girls, the film seems to say, this world was real. Their friendship had created this magic, and made possible the ultimate dream of every disaffected adolescent: to step out of their reality and into a newly expansive, transcendent one of their own conception.

Cocaine was our Borovnia.

Like Pauline and Juliet's imaginary kingdom, coke started as something Haley and I did casually, like all of our downtown fuckup friends did various drugs casually. But slowly—slow enough that we didn't notice at first—it took on a life of its own, until the world we inhabited together while high started to feel more real, more full of life and color, than the drab sober world we happily skipped away from, arm in arm.

Soon we spent nearly every day speed-walking around the

East Village, wiping our noses constantly, with pupils so dilated our irises disappeared. We walked straight up the center of the sidewalk, pedestrians parting to let us through, like we were alone in the crowded city. We bellowed Bob Dylan's "Like a Rolling Stone," L7's "Shitlist" and "Monster," looking at each other lovingly when we got to the line "My partner in crime, my insanity double." Mostly, while we walked, we talked—recounting every detail of our lives we could think of in rapid-fire sound bites.

When I remember those cocaine days, I remember them all together, like a multiple-exposure photograph of us pacing the neighborhood where we're on every street at once, hundreds of ghostly replica images of us walking up First Avenue and down Second and across Ninth Street—both in our leather jackets and thick black eyeliner, hands heavy with rings flying around in animated gesticulation. I remember the motion, as if we stood still and the neighborhood sped past and around us. The urgency of deciding it was time for a cigarette and looking for the right stoop (we always stopped and sat on a stoop to smoke, just one in a long, long list of things we always did in precisely the same way). Eventually we knew the best stoops on each street—they had to have more than one step, a high enough perch; and be recessed enough that we were slightly off the street, but not so recessed that they might have made a tempting spot for someone to piss in the night before.

I can see us so clearly: two pale girls dressed in black, skinny as street dogs, approaching a favorite stoop and both slowing down instinctively. Not even the briefest break in the torrent of stories we were volleying back and forth as we had a second, simultaneous conversation with only eyebrows or jutting chins, agreeing it was time for another smoke break. Smoothing the backs of our black handmade mini-mini-miniskirts as we sat, perching on the very edge of the concrete step, knees touching or almost touching as we angled ourselves toward each other, still talk, talk, talking so quickly, like we were on a phone line that was about to be cut. Taking our packs of Lucky Strikes out of the pockets of our leather jackets and tap, tap, tapping them against the heels of our hands exactly three times before each taking out a smoke and squeezing it between our lips, jittery with our jaws' stimulant clenching; flinging curtains of curly hair out of our faces. A few rare seconds of silence as we both focused on controlling the jerking, vibrating motions of our mouths and hands for long enough to get the cigarettes lit before shoving our matching black mini–Bic lighters back into our bras. I can see our bony knees bouncing up and down and up and down, fingers flick, flick, flicking ash off of our cigarettes whenever we weren't taking drags—which we did perfectly in sync. Sucking our smokes down to the filter and flicking them into the street in parallel arcs, before rising and continuing to pace the neighborhood, both aimless and hurried at once.

I remember the dizzying speed at which we walked, in lockstep like one creature with four combat-booted feet. I remember the way Haley's voice would go up in pitch when she was worked up about something, and the way she'd smack my shoulder when I teased her. I remember how we would free-associate from one memory to another, sometimes interjecting "Remind me: museum," or "School bus," or some keyword or phrase to help us remember the memory we were queuing up to share next.

I remember it all so well. Except for a single thing either of us said.

If my visual memory of those walks is a multiple-exposure photograph, my auditory memory is the sound of a thousand conversations happening at once, at double speed—so many words spoken over each other at the same time that none are intelligible. There are too many almost-identical memories for my mind to pull out a single one. But I remember the pitch and speed and urgency, the breathless excitement. The feeling of pouring into her as she poured into me, this very deliberate (if frenetic) act of *knowing* each other. It was like we were trying to catch each other up on every single experience either of us had had before we met, to approximate the feeling of having been through it all together from the beginning. With each new detail, I came closer to knowing her as well as I knew myself. To obliterating the border between us, as if we could enter each other's skin and replay each other's memories as our own. As if together, we could leave this plane of existence where just because we were born as two separate entities, we necessarily had to stay that way.

A photographer scouted us in the park for an editorial spread in *Purple* magazine, and when the issue came out, we didn't understand why Haley's mother was upset to see a published image of us in fishnets and matching burgundy bras, arms and legs intertwined and wrapped around each other, faces pressed together. We hadn't thought of the pose as suggestive—we were just being us, being close, encircling each other and holding each other up.

There was a physical intimacy inherent in coming to see each other as extensions of ourselves; a tangible way to demonstrate how thin the boundary between us was. We held hands walking down the street, and sometimes spooned in bed when we slept over at each other's apartments, and occasionally made out while dancing at shows, especially when we were on ecstasy. I never wanted to have sex with Haley—there was something too sisterly in our love to go that far—but I liked kissing her because I wanted us to be as close as possible. It was more like we were trying to consume each other, to be subsumed and share spit and breath. . . . It still sounds like I'm describing sex, doesn't it? But no, there were other girls I kissed because I was attracted to them; with Haley it was something else.

Much of the discussion about *Heavenly Creatures* and the real story that inspired it has centered on whether the two girls were lesbians. Journalists, biographers, and documentarians insist on a clear dividing line between an obsessive friendship and a sexual relationship, as if defining that boundary could change everything about the story. In the film, Juliet and Pauline's relationship is depicted as physically intimate, possibly sexual. They sleep wrapped in each other's embrace, kiss on the lips, bathe together; one scene shows them topless in bed as a voice-over quotes from Pauline's real-life diary: "We have now learned the peace of the thing called Bliss, the joy of the thing called Sin." The real-life Juliet, who became a famous crime novelist under the pen name Anne Perry, denied that there was ever a sexual aspect to their relationship, calling the suggestion "grossly offensive" in a *New York Times* interview shortly after the release of *Heavenly Creatures*, which she refused to watch.

Maybe Peter Jackson invented or exaggerated some of these moments to make a more compelling movie. Or maybe the real-life Pauline and Juliet did kiss and cuddle, but it wasn't sexual, just a way to express a depth of love too big to contain, too magnetic to express without physical touch. Or maybe a friendship can include a sexual element without that automatically becoming its defining characteristic. Regardless, it was this intimacy that stood out to me most the second time I watched *Heavenly Creatures,* at the height of my all-consuming love for Haley. This time, I was able to recognize elements of Pauline and Juliet's relationship as familiar, not just aspirational.

To be clear: Haley and I never killed anyone. But then again, no one ever tried to separate us.

Near the end of *Heavenly Creatures,* there's a black-and-white slow-motion scene of the two girls on the deck of a ship. They're smiling and running toward Juliet's parents, both calling Juliet's mother "Mummy." The girls kiss each other tenderly on the lips, smiling as they sail into the shared future they wanted so badly. It's an imagined scene, giving the viewer a glimpse of what "happily ever after" could have looked like if Pauline's mother had gone along with what the girls wanted.

But then the story continues. Instead of sailing away with one girl's mother, they take a fateful walk in the park with the other's.

Eventually, Haley and I stopped doing coke. The period of our lives that was defined by high-speed secret sharing lasted just a little more than a year, but it felt like several. When you're fifteen and sixteen, a year is a long time. An era. Especially when you've packed a decade's worth of sped-up conversations into it.

When the coke bubble burst, we started hanging out with some of our old friends again, though still making it very clear we were an inseparable unit. We told stories together, alternating lines like a couple that's been married for forty years. We always arrived together, and we left together so I could walk her home in time for her curfew.

Sydney's sixteenth birthday party was at the uptown penthouse apartment of a guy we knew, whose parents somehow agreed to let us take it over for the night. Haley and I got dressed and did our makeup together like always, and arrived at the party together, where a bunch of us dropped acid for the occasion.

A couple of hours into the party, I ended up locked in the pristinely white, calm, quiet bathroom with Raiona and two other girls. We were all tripping hard, and decided that the four of us, all blondes, were four quarters of Alice, from *Alice in Wonderland,* and we were safely in an isolated corner of the universe known as Alice's Bathroom. The party outside was overwhelming, but Alice's Bathroom was all cool tile and comforting echoes.

People knocked, but we told them to use the other bathroom, that this one was occupied. We stayed in there for hours, sitting on the floor, in the tub, on the closed toilet; smoking out the window and brushing each other's hair.

I completely forgot that Haley was out there, until a voice I didn't recognize called through the door that she was asking for me.

"I can't," I said. "I'm busy."

The other Alices and I were giving each other hand massages, wondering whether the world outside of this bathroom still existed. I didn't particularly care if it did, because I never wanted to leave anyway. The bathroom was a droplet of milk, we'd decided, floating in a universe of orange juice. We couldn't open the door, or else our consciousnesses would curdle. We shoved a towel under the door to prevent leaks.

A little while later, someone else came to the door and said Haley was really upset, crying, and she wanted me to come out. Normally, her crying was my cue to rush to her, to pay attention to only her. But I didn't understand why she'd want to rip me from this perfect porcelain womb. I didn't want to leave. I started to cry, too.

"It's okay if you want to stay," Raiona said.

"Yeah, you don't have to leave just because she wants you to," another Alice agreed.

They all nodded in unison, a chorus of "Yeah!" and "That's true," and six blue eyes blinking like a kaleidoscope.

This idea, that I could make a decision for myself rather than for "us," went against everything Haley and I had built—our own universe of two with our strict procedures for everything from when to leave a party to how to eat the single quesadilla we liked to share for lunch. I'd rejected rules in every other aspect of my life; my mother had given up on enforcing a curfew, I hadn't been in school in over a year, I shoplifted whatever I wanted. But I had followed our rules without question, and the most important one was to prioritize each other over anything and everything else.

But in that moment, in the safe calm of the clean white-tiled bathroom, I realized it was true—I could do something I wanted to do, even if it wasn't what Haley wanted—with the all-at-once acid-trip clarity you can almost hear ringing in your ears like a tuning fork.

It was a small fissure in our enmeshment that spider-webbed outward.

Slowly, at first just after Haley's curfew, I started spending more time with a group of guys we'd met in the park. Every night until dawn they smoked hand-rolled cigarettes and drank strong beer and cheap liquor, played guitar and argued over details of music history. I chimed in whenever a musician I'd heard of came up, and carried my weight when the conversation turned to books. They played shows in the West Village, and soon I was going to all of them, rapt with the notion that this bohemian New York City life still existed, and I could be part of it. I started getting weepy poetry drunk instead of angry yelling drunk, and told myself that this was growing up.

I liked the feeling of possibility that came with moving freely through a group, having different conversations with a dozen different people over the course of one bustling night. I wanted Haley there, too, but I wanted her to be one of many people I talked to, rather than the only one—or rather than being part of every conversation *we* had with anyone else.

The more my life expanded beyond the intense, singular focus Haley and I'd had on each other, the less appealing that kind of closeness became. I was figuring out who I was and discovering that I actually liked the person I was growing into, but this new confidence threatened our bond; it allowed me to stray from the little corner where we used to huddle together—the two of us against the world.

I had wanted an obliterating love, a love in which I could lose myself completely. To trade the solitude of my singular identity for a place to belong; one half of something larger than myself. I had wanted this, and somehow, miraculously, I had found it. For a while, it was everything I dreamt it would be. I never had to be alone with a single thought or doubt or fear because Haley was always there, ready to receive whatever was bubbling up in me. And whatever was left was washed away by what I received from her—displacing my own desires, anxieties, and grudges for hers. I never had to face indecision; I could just do what Haley wanted to do.

But the self is a tenacious thing. It will allow itself to be submerged, for a time, but there in the murky waters of love, or grief, or addiction, or fear, or whatever you try to drown it in—it waits. It waits for its moment, for the first crack in the surface, and then it struggles forth.

By the time Haley left the city for college, we still called ourselves best friends, but our inside jokes were all old now; references to a shared past rather than a current life together. We both made new friends, started to live separate lives. But there was still an urgency to our connection, a feeling that we had to constantly reaffirm for each other and everyone else that we loved each other most. We still talked on the phone several times a week, and slipped right back into our patterns during her first summer break—ignoring everyone else to hang out with just each other, doing our makeup together at her parents' apartment, singing along to all of our favorite songs. Only now we went to bars instead of walking aimlessly and chain-smoking on stoops—reveling in how our power multiplied when we were together, and never paying for a drink. I cherished these few months of being so intensely "us" again, knowing they were finite; that she'd go back to school and I would come down from the high of our communion.

The next year, Haley came home over a long weekend and picked me up at my college newspaper office, where I introduced her to my new school friends. She agreed to hang out for a little while so we could finish up work, and then we'd all go to a bar together. I was hopeful that she'd like these new people I was spending all of my time with; that I could have both worlds at once.

Almost immediately, sitting on one of the beige metal desks that lined the perimeter of the small third-floor office in the run-down liberal arts building, swinging her legs, Haley started playing the "Remember that time . . ." game, listing our most outrageous antics: "Remember that time we paid for a gram of coke with a bag of quarters?" "Remember that time you pulled a knife on that guy on the street when we saw him hit his girlfriend?" *Remember that time, remember that time, remember that time* . . . chiming in with a new anecdote each time conversation lulled as we all tried to finish what we were working on so we could leave for the day. I responded without enthusiasm, and my new, much more straitlaced friends just stared. Or worse, focused with extra intensity on their computer screens, trying to do me the favor of not staring.

Afterward, I couldn't shake the feeling that Haley's oversharing had been less about putting on a show for my new friends and more about putting me in my place—she was trying to remind me who I "really" was, or at least who she thought I really was. I felt the claustrophobia of being loved so fiercely for exactly who you are that to change is a betrayal.

I wasn't ready to let her go yet though. I still loved her, and I knew that she had saved me, that she had been the only stability in the hardest part of what was, whether I saw it that way at the time or not, still my childhood. I didn't know how to articulate that I wanted our relationship to settle into a new rhythm; to develop into a more grown-up best friendship with a little more space to breathe, without her hearing only "Leave me alone." So instead I told her later, when we'd left the group, "You know, I don't advertise all that shit."

If Pauline and Juliet's story hadn't ended so violently, if nobody had ever tried to separate them, would one of them have eventually tired of spending long hours imagining the wars and marriages of the Borovnian royal family, or decided they didn't actually like opera all that much anymore? How would the other girl have responded to such treachery?

There's no way to know, of course—it's like wondering whether Romeo and Juliet would have lived happily ever after if not for their ill-fated timing. It's only because these teenage love stories ended in tragedy at the height of their intensities that they're immortalized forever at full blaze. If *Romeo and Juliet* had a happy ending, it wouldn't have rippled through the ages the way it has. If Pauline and Juliet's obsession with each other hadn't driven them to murder, we never would have heard of them. There would be no movie about their love. They would be just another pair of teenage girls who loved each other obsessively, who built their whole identities in each other's eyes. Who each gave the other their very first taste of feeling seen and loved, as the versions of themselves they most wanted to be.

I tried for years to reconfigure my relationship with Haley into one that could last, trying to hold out until something finally shifted and settled into a new pattern. I remember these latter years as a constant effort to carve out a little bit of space for myself without losing her entirely; I imagine she remembers them as a slow abandonment.

By the time we were in our mid-twenties, Haley and I had been "best friends" for a decade, with about eight of those ten years spent struggling over how close was too close. This quiet battle finally came to a head at an L7 concert in Brooklyn. I bought a single ticket as soon as they went on sale, planning to go to the show alone. Seconds later I got a text from Haley saying that she got tickets and did I want to go together? I rolled my eyes and responded, "I'll just see you there."

As I entered the high-ceilinged anteroom of the venue, I spotted her almost immediately—we'd arrived at the same time, and were both still slipping ticket stubs into our pockets and looking around for the bar when we saw each other. We still dressed alike: black skinny jeans, black tank tops, black boots, black hoodies—better-fitting, less distressed versions of what we used to wear. We made small talk as we shuffled slowly forward in the long bar line, and I thought about how strange it was that conversation could feel awkward between us. Part of me wanted to search for our old connection, to take both of her hands in mine and say *Hey, it's me*, and let everyone else in the crowded space disappear around us. But I knew it was too late; that channel between us was closed.

When we both had our small, overpriced plastic cups of whiskey soda, dripping with condensation, we drifted to an out-of-the-way spot near the entrance to the main hall. I scanned the wall of T-shirts behind the merch table, looking for one I might want to buy, distracting myself from our strained conversation. Every word out of her mouth felt like a slight. The raised eyebrows and the tone with which she said "Oh wow, the Upper West Side, huh?" when I told her I was moving pissed me off, and as I heard myself saying "Yeah well, at least it's still in the city" with a passive-aggressive shrug, I wondered why the fuck I was engaging in this contest—I didn't look down on her for staying upstate after she graduated, but who the hell was she to judge me for leaving the old neighborhood when she'd left the city entirely? I felt disgusted with both of us for stooping to these catty barbs. After everything we'd shared, this was what was left? It was worse than nothing.

Finally the lights went down, cheers from beyond the double doors indicating that the band had come out onstage. I took the opportunity to say "Well, see ya!," quickly tossing what was left of my drink into a trash can and disappearing into the crowd alone rather than walking in together and getting stuck under this blanket of resentment for the whole show. I pushed my way to the front, screaming all the air out of my lungs as reverb from the opening chords echoed through the cavernous space. I danced and sang along to the whole set, reveling in the feeling of being one body in a crowd.

The next day, I sent Haley a text saying it was time to "drop the pretense" and admit that our friendship had been over for a long time. She responded "Fair enough," and that was that.

Talking on the phone late at night, Haley and I used to compete for the most over-the-top pronouncements of love—

declaring that we'd rather be "homeless with no teeth, living in a box on the street" than lose each other, we'd gladly give up every other friend for each other, we'd gouge our own eyes out for each other, and so on. The first few times I watched *Heavenly Creatures,* the murder at the end felt like those proclamations—a dramatic way to depict the depth of devotion.

When I watched the film again recently, though, now more than twice the age of Pauline and Juliet, the murder felt disturbingly inevitable. This time, I wasn't able to forget the bloody faces at the beginning.

There were a few moments—like an early montage of Pauline and Juliet's budding friendship that ends with them getting undressed in the woods, screaming the words to their favorite opera—that made me nostalgic for being so young and loving my best friend so much. I thought of me and Haley trading shirts in the middle of Tompkins, or the time she forgot to put deodorant on and we rubbed our pits together so she could take some of mine. I remembered how hard we used to make each other laugh—how absolutely fucking hilarious everything was when we were together. And for just a moment, I was tempted to text her, even though it had been almost five years since that L7 show, and we hadn't spoken since.

But those flashes of nostalgia, when the love between Pauline and Juliet still felt idyllic, were few and fleeting on this latest rewatch. What stood out to me this time was not just the intensity of the girls' feelings for each other, but the danger underpinning that intensity. The warning right at the start: Nothing good can come of this.

When the real-life Pauline and Juliet were eventually released from prison, it was on the condition that they have no contact with each other ever again. When I first learned this part of the true story, it felt tragic—I imagined them, grown women, longing for each other. Star-crossed. But it's clear now that there was no coming back from what they'd shared. No hope of just being normal friends who had been close once, when they were girls.

Kissing Girls

There was a perfect dive bar on the stretch of Houston Street between my apartment on Ludlow and the high school I attended with rapidly decreasing frequency. If I slept through first and second periods—which I usually did—the bar would be open by the time I walked east toward the river and toward school. And when trudging reluctantly toward a third-period class that I was definitely going to fail whether I showed up or not, music from the jukebox floating out of the bar's open door drew me in like the scent of a fresh-cooked turkey in a *Tom and Jerry* cartoon.

My eyes took several seconds to adjust as I stepped in from the bright late-morning sun, pushing my sunglasses up and back like a headband and trying to compose my face into an expression that said I belonged there. The first few times, the bartender with a buzz cut and tattooed, muscular arms asked for my ID, briefly squinting at my badly chalked fake before waving me in with a smirk. Then she stopped asking, greeting me instead with a nod. I convinced myself at the time that she actually believed I was twenty-two like my ID said, not fourteen.

There were usually just a couple of day-drinking regulars at the bar that early, and I'd saunter up and join them, affecting their grown-up blue-collar world-weariness that moved slower than my teenage eagerness. The windows on two walls of the bar, situated on a corner, were mostly papered over with posters advertising upcoming shows—music and an infamous bimonthly "Xena Night," complete with sword fighting and Lucy Lawless look-alikes—so the bright sun outside peeked through only in pinholes of light. During the day, the stage in the corner was bare and still. There were more posters covering most of the walls, and the faint smell of bleach from the end of the previous night, along with the ever-present smell of stale beer that could never quite be scrubbed away.

Women hunched over their beers or leaned sideways on the edge of the bar, chatting and laughing, and one of them almost always eventually offered to buy me a drink after I perched near them with manufactured casualness. All of the patrons were women—Meow Mix was a lesbian bar. This fact felt incidental to me then; the one bar that was on my way to school and accepted my fake ID happened to be a lesbian bar, so that's where I hung out. Never mind that I knew as soon as my eyes adjusted to the dim light which of the women sitting at the bar I most hoped would buy me a drink, drawn to a specific kind of hard-edged femininity that I wanted to both emulate and touch.

After an initial trepidation, and a first beer, I settled into a genuine ease, shooting the shit with these women about the new construction down the block, about the weather, about that idiot Giuliani, about whatever music happened to be playing and which bands we'd seen live and which bands we most wanted to see live before we died. And then I noticed the feeling of comfort, and it wobbled into something disorienting—

like when you pay too-close attention to how you walk and then suddenly you can't walk normally anymore.

There was always a certain awkwardness involved in drinking in bars so young, though I was pretty good at hiding it. An awareness of acting like you're not self-conscious, which is, necessarily, a kind of self-consciousness. But at Meow Mix I felt this dissonance doubly. Two distinct flavors of the same uncertainty, one minute being sure I was blending in, the next convinced that everyone could tell I didn't belong.

If I had been exclusively into girls, it might have been different. I might have gone to Meow Mix specifically because it was a lesbian bar, and being underage might have been the only thing that made me feel like I wasn't supposed to be there. But it was the early 2000s, and bisexuality was treated as either a sexual rumspringa on the way to one binary orientation or the other, or a way for girls to "act out"—less about desire and more about performing sexual adventurousness. If you were a lesbian, fine. That was legible and believable. But if you were a girl who usually or even sometimes hooked up with guys and then you hooked up with a girl, you were definitely doing it for attention.

I wanted to kiss girls for the sake of kissing them, not just to entertain or excite some male third party, or to be "wild" or show how uninhibited I was. Although I admit, I kissed plenty of girls for those reasons too.

My friends and I used to make "hookup charts," writing the names of all the girls we knew down one side of a piece of paper and all the guys down the other, and drawing lines between everyone who had ever kissed, or fucked, or drunkenly groped. We'd be sitting on a park bench or in a diner booth, or cross-legged on someone's bed, a spiral-bound notebook would appear and we'd squeal and exclaim over every improbable pairing all over again, as if we hadn't just played this game weeks or months earlier. We were entertained by how incestuous our large network of friends was—and by the fact that there were almost as many lines looping back along the left side of the page, from girl to girl, as there were crisscrossing from left to right. This is to say: I've made out with most of the girls I was friends with as a teenager.

But, we would have insisted then, it didn't really count.

My friends and I were immersed in counterculture in a progressive city, but the dominant culture's attitudes still seeped into our thinking—even Riot Grrrl and Anaïs Nin couldn't fully drown out the reactions to Britney and Madonna kissing at the VMAs.

The summer after I became a semi-regular at Meow Mix, there was a party, hosted by some friend of a friend of a friend whose parents were away for the weekend. I showed up with a small crew, and after we took over the iPod and commandeered a few bottles of liquor from the kitchen counter, I went out on the balcony for a smoke. As I searched for my lighter, patting my pockets with the free hand that wasn't holding my red Solo cup full of someone else's rum, a girl with long, shiny blond hair stepped toward me, cupped one hand around the cigarette between my lips, and lit it for me. I smiled and thanked her, and she smiled back, leaning against the railing next to me and saying her name like it was a full sentence. I replied with mine, mirroring her declarative tone, and we launched into the usual smokers' small talk.

She dressed like a guy—baggy jeans and a band shirt, filthy Converse and a wallet chain—but she had long eyelashes and smooth pink lips, and she held eye contact while we spoke in a way that made me trip over my words. When my cigarette was gone, I realized she had finished hers a while ago—had stayed to talk to me while I finished mine. I ground the butt against the railing and flicked it off of the balcony onto the street. She still didn't move to go inside. I didn't want to go in either, so I took out another cigarette and held the open pack out to her. She took one with a small, satisfied laugh, taking another step toward me to light my cigarette again before lighting her own. We stayed out there like that, talking about music and movies and the city, chain-smoking and standing closer and closer to each other, for hours. I heard myself laughing at everything she said, stopped even pretending to look for my lighter while she lit every cigarette for me, even after I found it in my hoodie pocket. I could feel that we were flirting, but I didn't know what to do next. Guys always made a move eventually, but she wasn't. So we just kept talking.

At some point my friends left, poking their heads out onto the balcony to say goodnight. When the music stopped playing inside and the host and a few stragglers started collecting discarded cups and bottles, the girl looked at her watch and said, "I guess we stayed out here all night," with a sly smile, and I thought for a second she was finally going to lean in. But she still didn't move—either toward me or toward the door.

"We could get a six-pack and go to the park," I offered, certain she would kiss me once we were alone in the grass. Her smile widened into a grin as she made an "after you" gesture.

I led her to the middle of the block on Seventh Street, where it was easiest to hop the fence into Tompkins without being spotted, and climbed over with practiced ease, reaching back for the bag of beer she'd carried from the store. She launched herself over the fence, wallet chain clanking against the metal, and landed with a thud and a laugh. I pointed toward my favorite spot—the green hill right in the center of the park, between two tall trees, where you couldn't see the street—and we made our way there. I loved the park at night, when it was closed and nobody was there except a few people sleeping by the chess tables—the grass and cobblestones lit by the soft warm glow of old streetlights, quiet enough to hear the trees gently rustling. We reached the hill and sat in the patchy grass, her cross-legged and me stretching my legs out and leaning back on my forearms.

She opened two beers with her lighter, and then started pulling up single blades of grass, twirling them around her fingers, sliding the smooth green sheaths over her chewed-on nails. I looked up at the sky, aware of her eyes on me, holding them there by extending my neck a little more, watching the dark branches swaying.

She asked if I had ever seen *Before Sunrise,* and I said no, even though I had, so she would describe the story to me—about two people who meet and fall for each other over the course of one long night.

Surely this was it.

And then instead of leaning toward me, finally, she started explaining how she'd hooked up with one too many straight girls, and it never worked out, and she just couldn't do that again. She was speaking generally—the way you might pointed-casually bring up a partner in conversation to let someone know you're not available—but I understood. I knew that she meant me, and I felt a flutter of panic, like in a dream where nobody can hear you speak.

Part of the feeling that making out with my friends "didn't count" was that there was usually an audience. Sitting or standing in a drunken circle at a party or a show, passing around a bottle or a blunt, someone would say something about who in the circle they had or hadn't kissed yet. And then, not an intimate connection between two people who were attracted to each other, but a collective swell: turning to kiss the girl next to you, and then the girl to the other side of you, and then the girl across from you. Only for a few seconds, tongues brushing lightly against each other, hands either kept to ourselves or placed stiffly on waists like at the middle school dances we considered ourselves so far beyond. Always followed by laughter. This wasn't serious, you see, it was barely even sexual—we were just free spirits, up for anything. And though we didn't acknowledge them, of course we knew the guys were watching.

But that night in the park—after hours of noticing the way the corners of her mouth moved just slightly into not quite a smile just before she spoke; of holding eye contact with her until I couldn't stand it anymore and looked away; of sitting close enough that all she had to do was lean toward me, just a little bit—nobody was watching. I didn't want her to kiss me because it would be funny or salacious or to prove I was fearless and bold. I wanted her to kiss me because I wanted to know if her lips were as soft as they looked; because I wanted to feel her hands, still fidgeting with blades of grass, find stillness on my back as she pulled me closer to her.

I wanted to object to her dismissal of me as one more dabbling straight girl, but in that moment, it felt like maybe she knew better. Like maybe my interest in girls had been a performance after all, and she had seen through it. But then why did I feel so crushed? And why did I hope she would change her mind?

I had no idea where performance ended and real desire began—there was no clear delineation between which girls I kissed because I was attracted to them and which just because, or to put on a show, or because it was one more way to feel close to my friends. But then again, at fourteen, fifteen, sixteen years old, I couldn't have made those distinctions when it came to the boys I kissed, either.

The truth is that every time I hooked up with a guy, there was some other desire at play beyond simply wanting that person: a desire to be desired, or to be the center of someone's attention, or to see what version of myself I might be with them, or to feel closer to someone I shared a lot of friends with but had never quite connected with directly, or to avoid the awkwardness or danger of turning them down. And of course, for all of our giggling, my girl friends and I wouldn't have been making out with each other all over the Lower East Side if there wasn't a current of real desire running through the display of uninhibited sexuality. But I was years away from even beginning to question the messages I had internalized about which desires were truly mine and which were affected for social currency.

—

The silence after she finished explaining why she didn't hook up with "straight girls" anymore felt different from every other silence between us that night—not charged with possibility, but cold with its extinguishment.

Hearing her describe me as straight and feeling myself recoil made it clear to me that she was wrong. But I couldn't yet articulate this clarity that was coalescing in my mind, in time with the first bit of light spreading across the sky. So I didn't say anything at all. I didn't correct her assumption about me. I just pulled out the lighter that I'd located hours earlier, and lit my own cigarette.

In Search of Smoky Cafés

New York City banned smoking indoors in 2003, the same year I became a chain-smoking, black-coffee-chugging high school dropout. I took this inconvenient timing as proof that I'd been born in the wrong era, nostalgic for smoky cafés filled with writers and artists surviving on grit and vision in a pre-gentrified city—nostalgic for a time before I was even born.

Instead of going to school, I painted and wrote and danced and drew and took artsy photographs with disposable cameras I shoplifted from Kmart. I visited the subterranean studios of random artists I met in the park and stayed up through the night and into the early morning, talking about what it means to live a creative life and how to stay true to what you believe in a world defined by making and spending money. I went to poetry open mics and punk shows in people's living rooms, and all of my friends were musicians or writers or both. I did a decent job of creating a bohemian life for myself considering the fact that the folk singers and beat poets of Washington Square Park had long ago been replaced with NYU students dressed like store-brand Paris Hiltons. But it felt impossible to be truly swept up in the artist's life when all around me gentrification was forcing closures of beloved cultural hubs and the ones that were left were lousy with loud, vacuous transplants shuffling around in their UGG boots. I hated the capitalist corrosion around me with a bitter passion only a teenage iconoclast can muster, and yearned for a nonspecific "more."

Then one spring day when I was fifteen, I saw Anaïs Nin's piercing eyes staring up at me from my favorite book vendor's table on Avenue A. I bought volume 1 of her diaries for three dollars without knowing anything about her and headed into the park, settling in to read Nin's stories about the artists and writers she spent her time with in Paris, having heated conversations about their work, about art in general, and life and love and all the big questions.

"Ordinary life does not interest me," she wrote. "I seek only the high moments. I am in accord with the surrealists, searching for the marvelous." She seemed to live a life that floated above drudgery—or as she put it, "monotony, boredom, death"—a life that was all silk and wine and art and sex and inspiration. She described the life I wanted more clearly than I had ever imagined it. And the backdrop for this magical life became the emblem of everything I desired, like it had for so many idealistic creative souls before me: Paris. Paris became shorthand for a world without all of the yuppie garbage that was cramping my outsider style in New York.

I understood of course that time had passed since the 1930s in Paris just like it had in New York, that many of the same problems likely existed there. But in a much more visceral way, it was easy to believe that the uncorrupted, smoky, jazz-filled utopia of Nin's Paris was a real place I could travel to if I wanted it badly enough. I dreamt of a world that was pure and raw and brutal and beautiful and full of surprise and wonder, never bogged down by trends and kitsch and mass marketing, and I was young enough to believe that such a world was possible.

One hot afternoon the summer we both turned sixteen, my friend Raiona and I started talking about traveling to Europe together. We'd go to Paris, of course, but also London and Amsterdam and Rome and Barcelona and a dozen other places that sounded romantic and far away. At first we talked about it like every other outlandish plan we'd hatched together since we met on the first day of high school and promptly started skipping classes together: the communal farm we were going to run upstate, complete with dance studio and library; the tenement building we were going to buy on the Lower East Side, where all of our friends could live for free; the art school that would be free to anyone and everyone, funded . . . somehow. But there was something different about this plan. Something that felt like maybe we could pull it off.

Just to see, we wandered into a travel agency and asked how much the cheapest tickets from New York to any city in Western Europe would cost. And then we spent the next two years saving our waitressing tips five dollars at a time, marking up one map after another, and emailing friends of friends and distant relatives who we might be able to stay with. We were determined to make this trip happen, but all along a part of me was waiting for the hitch, the disaster, the reason it would all fall apart. Traveling the world sounded like something other people did—rich people; or bohemians from bygone eras, like Nin and Hemingway and all of those long-dead icons who managed to survive on wits and pocket change. Not two working class teenagers in the early aughts waiting tables to pay for cellphone minutes and malt liquor.

But despite the seeming impossibility, we kept reminding ourselves and each other that they'd sell plane tickets to anyone—we just had to save the money. That meant living off of two-dollar falafel and pizza, not splurging on five-dollar diner breakfasts; smoking rollies instead of packs; shoplifting or sewing when we wanted new clothes instead of browsing thrift store sale racks. Whenever one of us wanted to buy something we didn't need, the other would start listing things we could spend that money on instead: baguettes, champagne, hostels! We made a game of it, playfully chiding each other into learning financial responsibility. Making the fulfillment of this ambitious dream something we owed to each other.

And then, somehow: Paris. Just in time to spend my eighteenth birthday eating chocolate and strawberry crêpes, smoking hash under the Eiffel Tower with some random French boys, and drinking red wine from the bottle while walking along the Seine. I described it in my journal (because of course, as a Nin devotee, I kept a detailed one) as "like a dream."

We saw flashes of Nin's Paris in an empty café where the surly waitress sat alone at a corner table reading a book, not looking up when we came in; in the aisles at Shakespeare and Company; in the twinkling lights around the Seine at night; in a beautiful white cat we followed down a side street and then around a corner and down another street, looking up to find ourselves completely lost. But those flashes were more often obscured by the hordes of tourists swinging armfuls of shopping bags from the same chain stores we had in New York, talking loudly in English and breaking the spell.

I tried to only see the Paris I'd dreamt of, but everywhere I looked was the same gentrification, the same advertisements, the same McDonald's and Sprint and H&M signs on beautiful old buildings that we'd hoped to escape. And very few groups of artists huddled in clouds of smoke. I tried to feel swept away, but there was a sinking disappointment below the surface, in the part of me that had genuinely hoped to time-travel.

Smoking indoors was banned in Paris in 2006—just a few months before Raiona and I arrived. Once again, I'd missed the boat. Of course, it wasn't only the smoky cafés themselves that I craved, but everything they represented: gathering places for people who didn't want to spend their afternoons shopping, communities built around creativity, places and people that let you escape the daily grind to sit still and talk about ideas and ask questions without answers. It was the idealized artist's life that I thought might have been a figment of my teenage imagination until I saw it reflected in Nin's diaries. And I didn't know where to find it if not in Paris.

As Raiona and I prepared to set off for the next stop on our trip, I felt dejected and aimless, like I had been betrayed by Paris or I had betrayed Anaïs Nin; like I really had been born at the wrong time, but there was nothing wistful about that notion anymore, it was just unfair.

Our bus to Amsterdam left at seven in the morning, so we decided to stay up all night and sleep on the bus rather than risk missing it, teenage late risers that we were. So on our last night in Paris, we set out with our big suitcases, with no plans other than to stay awake until sunrise.

We sat at a bar and nursed one glass of champagne each, trying to stick to our strict budget and knowing that drinking too much would make it harder to stay up all night. As bars started closing and nightlife dwindled to quiet, we set off wandering; smoking cigarettes by the Seine and taking photographs of empty streets. The streetlights were a romantic shade of yellow, and when the narrow, twisting side streets were empty of tourists they could almost have been the Paris we'd been looking for. We stood for a long time in front of Notre Dame, the gargoyles so much more magical and imposing in the dark and quiet than they had been when we first saw them a few days earlier, in the bustling daylight.

Around three-thirty, we were starting to drag, no longer exclaiming at every picturesque corner, tired of carrying our heavy bags. We saw a café up ahead and decided we could spare a few more euros for a place to sit and some caffeine to get us through the next few hours. Soon after our cappuccinos arrived, we noticed that too many people were coming up the stairs in the back for them to lead to the restrooms, as we had originally assumed. People were emerging sweaty and grinning, and it was clear there was something going on down there. We went to check it out and found a bouncer at the bottom of the stairs. We asked what was going on behind the door he guarded, and when he answered flatly "Cabaret," our eyes lit up. But then he continued: "Twenty euro each." That was more than we'd allotted to spend each day, and the cappuccinos had already put us over budget. We turned to go back upstairs, but, seeing our disappointment, the bouncer ushered us quickly through with a wink.

Inside was a cavernous space with stone walls which someone later whispered to us had once been part of the catacombs. The space was lined with picnic tables, crowded with people drinking and singing, and atop each table a mostly nude woman draped in feathers and beads danced to the lively jazz playing on the stage up at the front. The air was filled with cigarette smoke.

We stood at the entrance, aghast, for several seconds before people trying to come in behind us brought us back to reality. We squeezed in at the end of a bench and accepted our tablemates' offer to share their pitcher of beer, striking up a conversation with them during the lulls in the music. They were a group of locals, a writer and a few musicians, friends of the performers onstage. We talked about what it was like to make art in our respective cities, and enjoyed the show, Raiona and I periodically catching each other's eye in amazement. They asked us about New York, and I saw on their faces that they romanticized our city as much as we did theirs, and wondered if they would be disappointed if they visited. Or if, on their last night, they might find exactly what they'd hoped for.

This—a room full of people enjoying music and dance and booze and each other, singing and talking under a cloud of smoke, all in on a secret together—was exactly the kind of "high moment" Nin described living for, the Paris we'd dreamt of. I'd been so disappointed when we didn't step off the train in Paris and straight into a scene like this, but I realized finally that I'd been thinking about it all wrong. Part of what made this so spectacular was the way we'd stumbled upon it; that we could have missed out on this perfect last night, our moment alone with the gargoyles of Notre Dame and then this cabaret, if we'd just sat and waited for the bus instead of exploring the city in the middle of the night, if we hadn't questioned what was going on downstairs in the café, if we hadn't sought it out.

The Paris that Nin described was the world she had created: It was the people she surrounded herself with and the conversations she had—of course there had never been a time when the whole city was like that, but all along, the Paris (and the New York) I'd craved was there, available to those who knew how to look. The magic of Nin and her writing was not just in the world she inhabited, but in the way she saw it, and her determination to see it that way—"I am possessed by a fever for knowledge, experience, and creation," she wrote. I understood then that the kind of exultant, creative life where everything is art and the "monotony, boredom, death" of "normal" life is kept constantly at bay is not a place that can be traveled to, or a time I missed out on: It's a way of living and a way of seeing that Nin was a master of, and that I could be, too.

Throughout the rest of our trip—our next stop, Amsterdam, and then on through Germany and Italy, running out of money before we could complete our clockwise trajectory through Spain and Ireland—Raiona and I reveled in the small, perfect moments, collecting them like gems. The moments that felt like we were tapping into something special, the *high moments*. We cataloged them in our journals: drinking hash milkshakes and making daisy chains in Vondelpark; seeing a little German boy singing to himself in a playground in Wiesbaden, his face and hands covered in chocolate; an opera performance in an ancient coliseum in Verona.

"I want to be a writer who reminds others that these moments exist," Nin wrote, and for me she was—it just took a few years, a trip halfway across the world, and a long night of waiting up for a bus for me to really understand what she meant.

Sad Girls

As I walked into Heather's bedroom, my eyes went immediately to a postcard pinned to the wall by her bed. I'd sent it to her from Paris eight years earlier, when we were eighteen. On the front is a photograph of the full moon shining large and bright behind the Eiffel Tower; on the back, a continuation of a conversation Heather and I had before Raiona and I left to backpack around Europe—about how, halfway across the world from each other, we'd still be looking up at the same moon.

We were teenagers then, unabashed in our interdependence, used to seeing each other more days than not. The idea of two months apart required dramatic proclamations of love and remembrance. But time had passed, and in our twenties we saw each other more like once every few months, for a dinner at which we both insisted, "We should do this more." Heather had invited me over to this apartment in Inwood several times in the last year or so, but for one reason or another, the scheduling had never worked out. We kept promising each other, "Soon."

Now I was finally here, for the first time, to pack up her things. She'd been dead for a week.

Sydney, Raiona, and I had volunteered to accompany Heather's sister, Jenn, and their father, Sammy, on this solemn errand—tenderly folding Heather's clothes and packing them up for donation, trying to find and discard the drug paraphernalia before Sammy saw it, throwing out her toiletries and makeup. Before tossing it into the trash bag, I swiped one of her lipsticks across my lips, a kiss goodbye.

We each chose a few things to keep—talismans of her. I took a T-shirt that said "Very Fancy" on it, because I heard the phrase in the voice Heather put on when we pretended to be the old Jewish ladies we wanted to grow into. When we stood in as mothers for each other, admonishing each other to eat more, and not to forget a coat. I scanned the stacks of books teetering against one wall, not on shelves but layered like bricks, and a slim off-white spine called to me: Sylvia Plath's *Ariel*. It felt like a morbidly appropriate souvenir of this day. Later I discovered that Sydney had had a similar thought, and taken Heather's copy of *The Bell Jar*.

Heather was a definite Plath Girl as a teenager. I was too—just two of countless teenage girls since the '60s to proclaim our love for the bracing and violent *Ariel* poems, and *The Bell Jar*, Plath's fictionalized account of her first mental breakdown, suicide attempt, and institutionalization—a not-at-all-subtle way of making sure the world knew we were in pain. "I just really identify with Esther Greenwood," we'd tell adults: a threat. Claiming Plath was a way to elevate our teenage sadness from pedestrian and expected and cliché to literary, tragic, romantic. To tie our early-aughts angst to a dignified and important history.

Janet Malcolm described the appeal of *The Bell Jar* perfectly in *The Silent Woman*, her book on Plath and her biographers:

"The book has a surface puerility, a deceptive accessibility: it reads like a girls' book. But it is a girls' book written by a woman who has been to hell and back and wants to revenge herself on her tormentors. It is a girls' book filled with poison, vomit, blood, and volts of electricity." We were girls filled with poison, vomit, blood, and volts of electricity, so of course we loved it.

We were also teenage writers who took our work seriously, another layer of our identification with Plath, who published her first poems when she was still in elementary school. Not just Heather and me—a bunch of us girls carried notebooks with us everywhere, while most of our guy friends always had guitars with them. (I don't know why that was the gender divide among our particular group of downtown misfits, but it was: the girls were writers, the boys were musicians.) Heather and I used to trade notebooks late at night, when we felt brave enough, letting each other into our most private selves, admitting that we cared about something enough to want to be good at it, contradicting the "fuck the world" apathy we cultivated most of the time. We wrote little notes of encouragement and excitement in the margins of each other's stories and poems, and then flipped to the first blank pages we could find to write longer notes gushing about how much we adored each other. "Like sometimes violets grow in the desert or the Arctic, a splash of color in a barren landscape," one such note from Heather reads, "I am lucky to have met you in such a plain and beige sort of place like this."

The dynamics of our large group were always in motion—an elaborate minuet, all moving together, but rotating who was closest with whom at any given time. Sydney and Heather were best friends when Haley and I were best friends. (They made a zine together in which some of Heather's writing from that time has been immortalized—including "Ode to Holden Caulfield," a short prose poem that includes the lines "You're an atheist and it shows" and "O my contemptuous love, you poor hateful virgin.") There was a period when our two pairs were feuding, and we'd sit on opposite ends of the semicircle in Tompkins and talk shit about each other. The acrimony had to do at least in part with Heather and Sydney being concerned about how much cocaine Haley and I were doing—or, as we would have explained it at the time, being judgmental bitches.

But eventually Haley and I stopped doing coke and started drifting apart, and around the same time, Sydney's parents sent her away to a horrible militaristic boarding school for troubled kids (which she wasn't, really—at least no more than the rest of us. Less, even. She still went to class). Two halves of fractured pairs, Heather and I took each other's hands perfectly in time to the music.

"I consider you my blood, my own family, and my best friend," another notebook letter from Heather reads. I wrote similarly ardent declarations in hers—and that postcard from Paris.

When I think about the time when Heather and I were closest, I think of Sylvia Plath, and our own teenage poetry, and I think of Janis Joplin. Despite the fact that neither of us could carry a tune, Heather and I loved to get drunk and sing Janis Joplin songs at top volume. Her music came from the heart, and we didn't need to be good singers to feel that anguish, or to belt it out.

Janis and Sylvia were wildly different personalities—

Sylvia the dignified, refined, perfect housewife on the surface and blazing Lazarus on the page; Janis the loud, raucous party girl, lovesick troublemaker, blueswoman with an infectious giggle. But we made patron saints of them both—sad girl icons of the 1960s, the decade we were sure we should have been living in instead of the bleak, hipsterified post-9/11 era.

We liked a lot of the more recent sad girl icons too—I favored the '90s sad girls whose melancholy was shot through with *poison, vomit, blood, and volts of electricity*: Fiona Apple, Shirley Manson, PJ Harvey, Courtney Love. For the most part I was more angry than sad—at least on the surface. I was a porcupine of a girl, daring anyone to come close enough to be stuck. But under all of that anger was a deep and vast well of sadness. I was feral with grief over my father's death a few years earlier, but I didn't quite know it. I just thought I hated everything. Only when I was alone did I feel the roiling sorrow beneath the surface. Heather's sadness was out in the open, ever-present like the cigarette that was always either dangling from her lips or accentuating her gesticulations. She was unabashedly, brazenly sad. And when I joined her, laying down some of my armor to wallow, we had so much fun writing sad poems and singing sad songs that we sometimes forgot to actually be sad.

Together we were tapping into something that felt timeless and vast—a state of being that transcended our own era, and felt more appropriately rooted in a romanticized past. And so: Sylvia and Janis.

We egged each other on, singing louder and louder with each repeated "*Come* on" before full-on bellowing the climactic "Take it! Take another little piece of my heart now, baby!" We let our voices break as we leaned into each other, crooning, "But then who cares, baby, 'cause we may not be here tomorrow," running one song into another to create our own drunken medley. Swaying back and forth, relishing the pain-as-art.

Most of my memories of those teenage years blur together—day after summer day lying around in Tompkins or Washington Square, or holed up in some free crib or diner when it was too cold to hang out outside. I remember the sounds all together—laughter and music and several conversations at once—more than I remember individual moments. I remember alcohol warm in my chest and my cheeks, tobacco under my fingernails. I remember laying my head on laps, and I remember playing with the hair of so many friends who laid their heads on mine.

But there are a couple of days and nights that rise above the din, flashes of specific, clear memory. One of those is a night that the guys rented out a room at the recording studio Funkadelic, and Heather and I went along. The room was dark and felt cavernous even though it was small and cramped. Our friends making music, me and Heather leaning against a wall in the corner with everyone's bags and coats and empty guitar cases, passing a fifth of Southern Comfort back and forth and laughing until we almost peed. Our combat boots and fishnetted legs were tangled in a pile, and Heather's face was bright red—Chinese on her father's side, she got the most intense "Asian glow," her cheeks and forehead red and hot to the touch whenever she drank, her eyes watery. She was embarrassed about it, pouting whenever anyone pointed it out. But I loved how it made her look perpetually like she'd just screamed with full force. Which she often had.

During actual takes we were quiet—each with a notebook

in hand, writing each other notes, challenging each other's ability to keep from laughing out loud. During one of these brief periods where we had to shut up, I drew quick portraits of Matt, Mike, Miles, and Jonah while they played. But the rest of the time it was like a normal night, talking about whatever, cracking each other up, but with something heightened about it. I made a point of taking it all in, etching it into my mind so I could say "I remember when" if this band made it big one day. But it's not the band I remember most (it was short-lived, and most of those guys went on to make much better music on their own or with other groups), it's me and Heather in the corner: singing "Turtle Blues" until the guys shushed us because they were trying to hear themselves play something else entirely; cackling, doubled over, me falling onto her legs and her draping herself over my back until we were one creature roiling with laughter and the exhilaration of being young and free and loud, the corners of our mouths sticky with the sugary residue of SoCo.

We drank Southern Comfort that whole summer and fall because it was Janis's drink. She famously drank so much of it that the company sent her a fur coat—we saw this as just about as cool as you could get. It wasn't enough just to be drunk teenagers; we wanted to have drinking problems, to drink too much. To drink so much that a liquor company would notice and want to sponsor us.

The truth is, we loved Janis as much for her drunkenness as her music; Sylvia as much for her suicide as her writing.

We weren't the first or the last teenage girls to romanticize sadness and tragedy, of course. Before Plath there were Virginia

Woolf, Emily Dickinson, and the Brontë sisters, each with her own morose devotees. Before Joplin there was all of the blues. More recently, there was the "sad girl aesthetic" era of Tumblr—young women posting photos of themselves with mascara tears running down their cheeks, or black-and-white selfies in which they're staring mournfully into the distance, with quotes about depression and existential ennui for captions.

This digital wave of the sad girl is often traced back to Lana Del Rey's rise in popularity, a ripple effect of her despondent retro image. Del Rey also reached back to the '60s in curating her aesthetics of sadness—though more *Valley of the Dolls* than Janis Joplin. When her studio debut *Born to Die* came out in 2012, Del Rey, with her Bardot hair, perpetual pout, and Novocain-monotone voice, made a proclamation: Sad is sexy. And a new generation of budding sad girls agreed.

The social media sad girl has a very specific tone—the inherent vulnerability of expressing sadness coated in a protective gloss of sardonic humor and irony. Alongside the dramatic crying selfies, sad girl Tumblr pages were full of simple, morose statements like "I hate my life" written in glittery pink cursive or pastels, the cheerful presentation clashing with the message to strike the discordant note central to so much internet humor. The depression humor of the online sad girl quickly spread beyond Tumblr. Emblematic sad girl Twitter account @sosadtoday skyrocketed in popularity, with each half-earnest, half-ironic post about anxiety and depression being retweeted more than the last—sentiments like "sometimes i remember i exist and i'm just like 'gross'" and "Mother's Day Card: Mom, I didn't ask to be born." The very first tweet on the account, in 2012, said only, "sad today." The poet and writer behind the account, Melissa Broder, later published an essay collection also called *So Sad Today*, broadening the reach of this particular flavor of sardonic melancholy even further.

The popularity of the online sad girl aesthetic prompted a wave of think pieces with titles like "When Did It Become Cool to Be a 'Sad Girl'?" and "How the Sad Girl Movement on Tumblr Might Be Making Light of Mental Illness." Many of these were the kind of hand-wringing and condescension you'd expect regarding a trend that was primarily the purview of teenage girls, but there were also legitimate concerns about whether the sad girls of Tumblr encouraged self-harm, and about the significant overlap between their aesthetics and the twisted "pro-ana" corner of the internet, where young women encourage each other's eating disorders.

On the other end of the spectrum, artist Audrey Wollen, who coined the term Sad Girl Theory as a framework for her photography and general creative philosophy, argued that expressing sadness could be a form of resistance to the expectation that girls be pleasant and pliable all the time. Wollen, who re-created famous paintings with nude or nearly nude photos of herself in a series posted to Instagram (keeping with the social media origins of the aesthetic even while elevating it), referred to the ostentatious sadness of Tumblr girls, and famous sad girls like Plath and Del Rey, as "an act of protest" and "an alternative to the hyper-positive demands of contemporary feminism" in a 2014 interview with *i-D*. (This was before #MeToo, and the Supreme Court's evisceration of Roe v. Wade, and feminism's return to rage. It's almost hard to remember a "hyper-positive" feminism now, but it rings a bell, as if from far away, that sounds like the word "empowerment.")

"I think it's important to look very hard at anything that mass culture wants to stay invisible," Wollen said in a 2015 interview with *Nylon*. "The number-one cause of death globally for girls between 15 and 19 is suicide, and yet, we still tell every girl that her sadness is individual, her own failure, her own symptom, and to keep quiet about it. Suffer alone." (In the years since, suicide has cycled in and out of that number one spot alongside complications of pregnancy and childbirth.)

A decade before Wollen articulated her Sad Girl Theory, before Tumblr or Instagram or Twitter existed, Heather and I were pushing against these same expectations that sadness be kept private. We were discovering the power in suffering together rather than alone. And our sad girl saints gave us a safe container into which to pour some of our too-big emotions, language to describe what we were feeling, and reassurance that we weren't the first to feel it.

When I got home from packing up Heather's apartment, I wrote "Heather's" on the title page of her copy of *Ariel* in small, neat script, as if I could forget. I started to read it, but only got as far as "Lady Lazarus," five poems in—to the line about meaning to "last it out and not come back at all"—before the connection to Heather felt too painfully literal. I closed the worn paperback and slid it onto a shelf, next to the notebooks full of my teenage ramblings interspersed with letters from Heather, where it would sit unopened for years.

Ariel, famously, was first published two years after Plath's death, after being heavily edited by her husband, Ted Hughes, from whom she had been separated. When her body was discovered early on a February morning in 1963, the *Ariel* poems as she intended them to be published were sitting on her desk in a black binder. Hughes removed twelve poems that Plath biographer Heather Clark describes as "personally damaging to him"—written during their separation, about his infidelity and cruelty. To replace the poems he cut, Hughes added thirteen others. He also changed the trajectory of the collection, making it feel even more like, as he would refer to the title poem years later, "a prophecy of suicide."

"Plath had ended *Ariel* with the hopeful poem 'Wintering,' whose last word is 'spring,'" Clark notes in her Pulitzer Prize finalist biography *Red Comet: The Short Life and Blazing Art of Sylvia Plath*. "The last three poems Hughes chose for the first edition of *Ariel*—'Contusion,' 'Edge,' and 'Words'—suggested, instead, depression and suicide. Because Hughes had omitted many of the fiery, taunting poems aimed squarely at him [. . .], the tone of Hughes's *Ariel* was bleaker than Plath's original manuscript." He'd sanitized her anger, transformed it into a more acceptably feminine sadness.

While Wollen wasn't wrong that society expects girls to swallow their sadness, sadness is still tolerated in a woman far more than anger. An angry woman is dangerous, unpredictable, uncontrollable. She must immediately be punished, shamed, or medicated back into complacency. Anger aims outward, disrupting systems and inconveniencing those in power, whereas we tend to turn our sadness inward, on ourselves—not bothering anyone or making a mess.

As the sad girl aesthetic illustrates, sadness can be neatly folded into a fragile, docile ideal of femininity when it's performed in the right way, by the right kind of woman. Which is to say: Sadness is the kind of transgression that is permissible for young, pretty, thin white women. The sad girls of Tumblr were mostly waifish, delicate, conventionally beautiful white girls—such that this supposedly subversive ethos often just reinforced the same narrow standards of who's deemed desirable as the mainstream fashion and film industries.

The right kind of sad girl is an iteration of one of the oldest feminine tropes there is: the damsel in distress. A sad girl is still lovable, because a sad girl can be rescued.

Until it's too late.

A sad girl whose sadness consumes her becomes a tragic, romantic figure. She becomes her pain, and her pain becomes a thing we wrap ourselves in and claim. She becomes an emblem, a vessel, a warning. A patron saint for the next generation of sad girls to worship and emulate. And in the process, her complexity and humanity are annihilated. The joy she felt in her life—the love Janis had for her dog, the delight Sylvia felt in sunbathing on a hot day, Heather's Shabbos dinners—is lost.

Thanks at least in part to the self-serving manipulation by her executor, it is this narrow archetypal sad girl version of Plath that catapulted, after her death, to the fame and recognition she'd sought while alive. *Ariel* sold fifteen thousand copies within ten months of its UK release and has sold hundreds of thousands since. *The Bell Jar,* originally published during Plath's lifetime under a pseudonym, was rereleased under her real name after her death, selling millions of copies and becoming a cornerstone of many a depressed teenage girl's identity.

"The public perception of Plath as a witchy death-goddess had been born and would not soon die," Clark writes. The tragedy of her death mingling with the brilliance of her poetry made Plath an icon, but it also made her sadness and her tragic end her defining traits. It wasn't until decades later that a new generation of Plath scholars would advocate for dimension in readings of her work—pushing fans to celebrate her birthday rather than her death date, publishing analyses and close readings of her poems about bees rather than only the ones that evoke death and violence.

Malcolm put it bluntly in *The Silent Woman:* "It has frequently been asked whether the poetry of Plath would have so aroused the attention of the world if Plath had not killed herself. I would agree with those who say no."

I don't want to flatten Heather in this way—as sure as I am that she would absolutely relish the title "witchy death-goddess." It's too easy to remember her as a sad girl because of her sad death. To rewrite her life, starting with the end. But there was so much more to her than that.

She carried herself with the ease of a beautiful woman, swinging her hips and not blushing at raunchy jokes, when the rest of us were still awkward girls.

She had this guffawing laugh—not the cackle that cracked the air around her when someone else said something funny, but a single goofy exhaled chuckle, the laugh she laughed after *she* said something she thought was funny. It was so totally incongruous with the hot girl it emanated from, so unexpectedly and endearingly dopey, you couldn't help but laugh at her laughing at her own joke.

She was proud of being Jewish and proud of being Chinese and she delighted in the exploration of both sides of her heritage, through study and food and fashion—cooking noodle kugel in a qipao and calling herself a "Lower East Side special." She traveled to Israel and to China, and brought back gifts for everyone from both trips.

She started going to temple regularly in her early twenties, memorizing all of the major prayers. And she taught herself Hebrew—all on her own, with books and flash cards. She was smart as hell.

She befriended a guy she met at temple who was in the process of leaving the Orthodox community and made it her personal duty to help him navigate entry into the secular world. That was another thing about her—she could, and would, make friends with anyone, anywhere.

These are the things I most want to remember about Heather.

But the sadness was such a big part of who she was, of how she saw herself and how she moved through the world, it would be as much a disservice to her to gloss over it as it would be to let it take over my memory of her completely.

The first time Heather called me in the middle of the night saying she wanted to kill herself, I treated it like an emergency.

We were two high school dropouts struggling to adjust to professional young adulthood. She was a legal secretary and I was a magazine fact-checker, but our nights of sitting on a stoop, drinking whiskey and crying on each other's shoulders, felt recent enough to touch, like we'd walked straight from one of those long nights, dazed and dehydrated, into our respective offices. We talked often about the awkward, unnatural feeling of slipping into the straight world after rejecting it so vehemently—afraid it would turn around and reject us right back.

On top of this strained transition, Heather had recently been diagnosed with bipolar disorder. The diagnosis reoriented what her sadness meant; made it something to be not just expressed but managed, tended to vigilantly with the help of professionals. It brought into stark relief the difference between being a sad and angry teenager, as we all had been, and being actually, clinically depressed. It had been hard to tell the difference when we were sixteen, singing sad songs and drinking too much sugary liqueur, crying over each other's sad poems and worshiping at the altars of our sad girl saints. But now the difference was clear: Heather's was a bigger, scarier sadness. It was a current she had to fight constantly, or surrender to and be swallowed forever.

I woke up to my phone buzzing on the table next to my bed, confused. It was past three in the morning. I blinked the sleep from my eyes and cleared my throat before answering urgently, "Hello?"

On the other side of the line, Heather sobbed.

"What is it? Are you okay? What happened?" I was up and out of bed now, pulling pants on while holding the phone between my cheek and my shoulder, ready to get on the subway and rush to wherever she was. My mind raced with everything horrible that could have happened: Was she in the hospital, a police station? Had something happened to her dad?

When she finally spoke, it was more of a wail, "I wanna die!" the last word drawn out and devolving back into sobs.

I offered to come to her, asked if she wanted to come to me, asked if I should call an ambulance, but I realized quickly that she didn't want to be rescued, she just wanted to be heard. She wanted someone to know how much she was hurting. So I listened. I got back into bed and lay down, but didn't close my eyes.

"I love you," I said. "I'm so glad you're alive. I'm so sorry."

Eventually her sobs slowed to sniffles. I asked if she thought she'd be able to sleep and she sighed, "Yeah." When I woke up again a few hours later, there was a text from her: "Thanks. Feeling better. Love you. <3"

But that call was just the first of many.

They all played out the same way, but after the third, or fourth, or twentieth time over the next few years, my responses lost some of their urgency. I stopped fearing that her life was truly at stake and came to understand the calls to be a release valve. They became routine. Then they became overwhelming. I started to run out of ways to tell her to go back to therapy, to take her meds; to reassure her that she was loved and yes, she would be missed if she died—desperately. I could sense her wariness, not wanting to give me more of her pain than I could handle. I would never stop taking her calls, but she could tell they were wearing on me, that I didn't know what else to say.

Eventually, the calls stopped.

I learned after she died that I was one of several people who got these calls—she rotated between us, trying not to dump too much on any one person. But still, one by one, we'd all burned out. We all reported the same thing to each other, after: "Eventually, she stopped calling."

Heather and I drifted apart in the last year of her life, when we were both twenty-six. I felt guilty for it even then, but I was on my own tightrope, trying to build a real life, and I didn't feel capable of catching her as she fell. It didn't feel like the end for us, though. We'd gone through periods of less frequent contact before, but I'd never stopped feeling the invisible tether between us, the connection that allowed us to snap right back into intimate closeness after months of being busy with our own lives.

The last time we saw each other, we had dinner at a Greek diner in Astoria. We ate lemon potatoes and so many dips we needed a second small table between us, and shared a carafe of red wine. We sat by the window, the late-summer evening sun glowing golden around us. We toasted her recent promotion at work and her plans to go back to school, and we talked about the book I was writing—my first reader, still cheering me on. We talked about clothes—how buying yourself something pretty to wear could make you feel more in control of your life, how it was an act of optimism to shop for yourself. But also how neither of us had found a way to escape the working class guilt of spending money on anything unnecessary, just in case a crisis was around the corner.

"Retail therapy is cheaper than regular therapy if you know how to find a good sale," she said with her goofy laugh, and we clinked our glasses of wine. There was no sign of the recent distance between us as we ordered a second carafe and conversation flowed from the trials and triumphs of the present to the possibility of the future and the ache of the past, all threaded through with laughter and warmth.

I assumed it would always be like that, each ebb eventually followed by a return. That we'd always be looking up at the same moon.

Janis Joplin's last album, *Pearl*, was recorded during the final weeks of her life—a posthumous work, like *Ariel*. It was her second album in the two years since she'd left Big Brother and the Holding Company at the end of 1968.

Janis stayed off of heroin for five months in the summer and early fall of 1970, while touring with her new band, Full

Tilt Boogie, and even restricted herself to just a couple of drinks a night to protect her voice. Until she ran into her old dealer at the hotel she was staying at in L.A., and relapsed. She died of a heroin overdose early in the morning of October 4, 1970.

After her death, the band and their producer, Paul Rothchild, returned to the studio to re-record some instrumentals and splice together what they had of Janis's unfinished vocals. Rothchild added her spur-of-the-moment recording of "Mercedes Benz" as the last track—ending with Janis saying, "Well, that's it!" and laughing her scratchy giggle. That closing line, like so much of Plath's *Ariel,* feels like it was spoken by a ghost.

Also like *Ariel,* it was this haunted work that truly cemented the artist as one of the greats. Released three months after Janis's death, *Pearl* was by far the most commercially successful album of her career, eventually selling more than eight million copies. "Me and Bobby McGee," one the three singles off of the album, stayed at number two on the charts for two weeks.

The original *New York Times* review of *Pearl* notes, referring to "Me and Bobby McGee," "It is somewhat eerie to hear her sing that song's chorus ('freedom's just another word for nothing left to lose . . .')" in the context of her death. As I read this review and imagine people listening to *Pearl* for the first time months after Joplin's death, Janet Malcolm's assertion that Plath's poetry wouldn't have made the impact it did if not for her suicide echoes in my mind. The situations are not exact parallels—Janis was already famous when *Pearl* came out, she'd been on magazine covers and performed at Woodstock. She was already primed for this to be her breakout album. But still. It's impossible that her death didn't add weight to the album, didn't make the sad songs sadder and the more upbeat ones bittersweet. That her death didn't infuse the public reception of *Pearl*, making people even more inclined to see it as a masterpiece, emphasizing the tragedy of her death right when she was doing her very best work—as Sylvia noted she had been in a letter to her mother shortly before she died.

Tragedy makes us cherish a person more. And when that person was a sad girl in life—a blues singer or a writer of confessional poetry, or a friend who romanticized her own depression—tragedy cements them as a symbol, a cipher to be decoded. They become a metonym for the very idea of sadness; a witchy death-goddess rather than a human woman who lived and died.

I am perpetuating this pattern while I name it, I know. My motivation to dissect and understand the sad girl trope doesn't absolve me of contributing to it. I'm mythologizing Heather, examining her pain because it killed her, even though I didn't pay enough attention to it while she was alive. I'm writing this now as a kind of penance, shoving my callousness in my own face. Or maybe I'm writing to understand how I could have missed what was right in front of me.

In the months before her death, when she'd run out of people to call in the middle of the night, Heather started venting her sadness on Instagram instead. She posted frequently, mostly memes about mental illness and extreme close-ups of her face, bleary-eyed like she'd been crying. Slack, expressionless. Wearing too much makeup. Her posts made me uncomfortable.

I didn't identify so much with the sad girl anymore by then. Partly because I genuinely wasn't as sad as I had been—at least not in the layers of consciousness close enough for me to access. And partly because when I got it together and went to college, I very intentionally left a lot of myself behind. I didn't want to show up in the world as a weepy, drunk, dirty street kid. I was ready to be an adult, ready to be so hypercompetent nobody would ever be able to tell there were pieces missing. Instead of snarling anger, I deflected with ambition and savvy. I still listened to Janis Joplin, but I didn't sing along with abandon anymore; when anyone asked what my favorite novel was, I said *East of Eden,* not *The Bell Jar*. I left the sad girl behind, a relic of my youth when everything was heightened.

Heather didn't.

At the time, the fact that she wanted her sadness to be seen made me take it less seriously. I thought she was playing into an image, and I didn't worry too much. That was just Heather being Heather. I might even have referred to her posts dismissively as a "cry for help." Now I see how fucked up it is that when we see something as a cry for help, we dismiss it rather than . . . helping. Now I remember that when we were teenagers telling adults how much we related to Esther Greenwood, trying to drink so much we'd get a free fur coat or at least make someone worry, we weren't just trying to rub it in people's faces—we were sending out a test signal. We were seeing if there was anyone there to answer the call when it was truly a matter of life or death, or if we were really as on our own as we felt.

But by the time we were in our mid-twenties, I felt like Heather should know better, or have more control, or be more careful what she put out in the world. We'd posted all kinds of dark shit on our LiveJournals back in the day, sure—but Instagram was different, less anonymous. And we were adults now, with professional jobs. I also didn't yet fully understand what her bipolar diagnosis meant; how much was out of her control. I judged her for being such a mess.

Layered over that visceral reaction was a more conscious understanding that I was wrong—that she could post whatever she wanted—and I didn't like myself for judging her. So rather than staying in the cycle of having a knee-jerk negative reaction each time I scrolled past a new lurid selfie and then feeling guilty for recoiling, I unfollowed her. (This was before Instagram had a "mute" option.)

Of course, after Heather died, I wanted to go back and scroll through all of those selfies, to examine them like clues, to see if maybe there was a caption that would feel like a message from beyond death, like Plath's "Dying / Is an art" or Joplin's fervent encouragement to "cry, cry baby." But she'd locked her account, so I couldn't. It took seven years for me to swallow my guilt and ask Sydney to take screenshots of some of Heather's posts and send them to me.

I remembered Heather's feed as one bleary-eyed, desperate-looking selfie after another, hard to look at and hard to look away from. But in the month before she died, I notice when Sydney sends me a folder full of screenshots, there were only a few of these. I find them beautiful now—not for their tragedy, but just because they're my friend's beautiful face. They don't look as dramatic as I remembered. Interspersed with these selfies is a perfectly normal-looking amalgam of glimpses of her life: a sign for evening services at her synagogue, a spread of new paints, a David Foster Wallace meme, a tattoo she liked of a sloth's face and the words "Live slow, Die whenever," and an absolutely stunning black-and-white photograph of her in which her hair is curled and her eyebrows darkened, and she looks like a Wong Kar-wai heroine.

Twelve days before she died, she posted a smiling photo of herself with the caption "One week. Different world. Different mood. Different me. Living proof. Things do get better." I scanned back through her posts and saw that seven days earlier she'd posted two depressed-looking selfies: one of her in bed, her hair covering her eyes, her mouth slack; another of her holding a cigarette, staring blank and expressionless past the camera. But it's the smiling "Things do get better" post that gets me in the gut. To see that she was trying, that she had hope, even, just twelve days before she decided there would be no hope for her ever again. In this picture, she's smiling, but her eyes are glassy, with dark circles under them. I can see the strain, the effort it took her to feel optimistic. Or maybe I can only see that now, looking back, knowing she'd be dead less than two weeks later. Would Plath's reference to carbon monoxide in "A Birthday Present" ("Sweetly, sweetly I breathe in") feel as ominous if you didn't know she died exactly that way soon after writing it?

I know that Heather's Instagram isn't a work of art on par with *Ariel* or *Pearl*. But it was a hurting woman's connection to the world; it was how she expressed herself. And now it's an archive rich with posthumous meaning. So I don't think the comparison is that much of a stretch, actually.

—

On Thanksgiving Day 2014, four days before she died, Heather posted ten times in a single day (before that she averaged more like once a day), almost all throwback pictures ranging from a year or two old to a couple from way back in the day—the Heather I recognize the most intimately. They're all happy pictures, a lot of sunshine: Heather hula-hooping at a music festival; Heather smiling with a view of Jerusalem behind her; Heather posing with her family dog; Heather sharing a margarita with her ex, drinking from a single glass with two straws, like a '50s malt shop image. Like she was feeling nostalgic, reminding herself of good times. If I'd still been following her then, and seen this flurry of images, would I have commented on one of the ones I recognized? It feels, now, like that's what she was asking for—for someone to say "Yes, I was there, I remember—you've been happy."

Or maybe she was consciously curating the last public images of herself, pushing the morose selfies down on her feed.

The last post in that flurry—also Heather's last post ever—is a meme, white text against a dark purple background: "i put the hot in psychotic." A decade later, this meme and the bleak black-and-white selfies are clearly recognizable as pitch-perfect examples of the sad girl aesthetic. Heather didn't have a Tumblr account, as far as I know, but she embodied the aesthetic on her Instagram right at the time when it started to spill over onto that platform and others beyond its birthplace.

Today, the once-controversial jokes of the online sad girl are ubiquitous far beyond their original little corner of the internet, with people posting casually about depression and dissociation on their otherwise professional Twitter accounts. There's even a perceived valor in doing so—sometimes the tweets are jokey and self-deprecating, but often they take an earnest tone and are accompanied by the hashtag #TalkingAboutIt. Writer Sammy Nickalls started the hashtag in 2017, explaining in a blog post, "Staying silent about my struggles, especially when I'm able to speak up without facing consequences, was just contributing to the stigma surrounding mental health. I vowed to be open about my mental health using the hashtag #TalkingAboutIt, and I encouraged my followers to do the same."

The Reddit group r/depressionmemes—a mix of the general "lol life is pain" brand of memes you can expect to find on other social media, and posts that directly express, if in meme form, suicidal ideation—has tens of thousands of members. And the sad girl lives on in yet another generation on TikTok, where #SadTok videos of (still pretty, young, mostly white) girls looking into the camera as tears roll down their cheeks have millions and millions of views.

When Heather and I loudly proclaimed our misery as teenagers, we were signaling our separation from the herd, our rejection of the social standard. Declaring that we saw the world clearly enough to see how fucked up everything was, even if the powers that be didn't want us to notice. But these sentiments aren't subversive anymore—they're almost assumed as a baseline.

This sense that everyone is depressed feels like it's at least in part a reaction to the political climate and the literal climate of the last few years; the pervasive feeling that the world is ending, for real this time. Impending fascism, global pandemic, daily mass shootings, and frequent catastrophic weather events have primed us all for malaise. And there's something cathartic about how normal it feels now to say out loud that everything feels hopeless and you're not sure you're going to live much longer. But I also can't help but think of Heather these days when I see one internet acquaintance after another post about being too depressed to cook—not as if this were a dire state to be in, but as a casual way to ask for recommendations of easy recipes; or express their enjoyment of new music by any of the new guard of sad girls like Mitski, Lucy Dacus, and Phoebe Bridgers by posting about how hard they're crying. It all feels so normal that it doesn't worry me at all. But the fact that it doesn't worry me sometimes worries me. If jokes about wanting to die are so casual now, how are we supposed to know when somebody means it?

The internet makes it difficult to tell what's real. This is a common conversation in terms of presenting only our most manicured selves, especially on Instagram—the most aspirational of the mainstream social media platforms. The prevalence of posts about depression feels like a reaction to the too-perfect online aesthetic that developed with the rise of influencers. People are rejecting the shiny illusion and trying to show each other that sometimes our hair is dirty and our desks are cluttered and our coffee doesn't have little foam hearts on it; that sometimes we even want to die. But even when people try to post about the messy, ugly, real stuff, it still feels like a manicured presentation. Like it's all still curated and put on for consumption, another lever to pull in adjusting how we want to be seen by the world. So much so that even a depression that will soon lead to suicide can feel, through the filter of social media, like content.

Heather wasn't just sad, she was bipolar, prone to severe

depression. We all knew this, but because being a sad girl had been part of how she presented herself to the world for so long, it seemed like she could go on posting mental illness memes and putting "Ball and Chain" on the jukebox at the bar forever and ultimately she'd be okay.

Heather died on the first day of December. We waited until the earth thawed the following spring to visit her grave, so we could plant flowers. Her sister, Jenn, picked us up in Manhattan—Raiona, Sydney, and me—and we drove together out to the Jewish cemetery in New Jersey.

I knew it would be hard, but I had intellectualized the idea of a grave, reminding myself that the physical remains are not the person. Heather is in my memories of her, in the sound of her laugh that I play over and over in my head to make sure I never forget it, in the places we used to go to dinner together, and in the songs we used to sing, the notes she scrawled in so many of my notebooks, always signed with a now-painful "Forever, —Heather." She's not in a box under the ground.

After driving the winding route through the cemetery, Jenn stopped the car. Raiona and I looked at each other across the backseat and both exhaled slowly before unlatching our seatbelts and opening the doors. Jenn was already out of the car and sobbing softly when we stepped out into the boomingly bright sun. The sky was an almost fluorescent blue, the grass spray-paint green. We were far enough inside the cemetery that we couldn't hear traffic. Without even a light breeze to rustle the leaves, the silence rang loud and sharp, as heightened as the too-bright sky, the perfectly warm but crisp spring air, cut through only by Jenn's low moans and my own abnormally resonant breath.

Jenn crumpled next to an uneven rectangle of dirt, the only grave in the section too new for grass to have grown over it, with no stone set in yet. As soon as I saw it, so anonymous, so haphazardly filled in, the tears came. I understood then that the grave site is not the person, but the symbol of their having been loved. To see Heather's looking so bare, it felt like she had been tossed aside and forgotten. I felt a desperate need to make it visibly clear that she was in fact loved, missed, remembered.

As we turned over the dirt and planted a row of tulips, then a row of hyacinths and daffodils, I felt an immense relief. We were performing the physical act of missing her.

Heather was no longer looking up at the same moon as me, maintaining our unspoken bond of friendship. Without her participation, that quiet awareness wasn't enough. And there, with my hands deep in the dirt making room for each bulb, reaching into the ground toward her, I knew it hadn't been enough when she was alive, either.

It felt good to perform this act of care for her, but I wished I had done a better job when she was alive.

Sitting in the car on the way back to the city, all of us silent, staring out at the too-perfect day and thinking our own thoughts about Heather, I glanced down and saw the dirt under my nails. I wanted it to stay there forever, a reminder to tend my friendships, no matter how strong the unspoken bond; to show I care, before the only thing left to do is plant flowers.

How to Support a Friend Through Grief

---

1. Suffer a tremendous loss early in your life. Perhaps the death of a parent at such a young, pivotal age that grief becomes a central part of who you are. Your homeland. Become comfortable in grief, learn its coastlines and caves intimately, so that when someone you love arrives on its shore, stunned and choking, you can greet them and show them around. Like when you and Carly met in college, when she was new to New York, and instead of the usual bars near school you brought her to Red Hook to see your old friends play music, and you stayed long after the bar pulled down the gates and started letting everyone smoke inside. Sharing your secret spots.

2. Let this friend support you through a second major loss of your own. When Sabina died the summer before your senior year, Carly came and sat with you on the fire escape. Her presence was steady and calm. You felt a little better with her there, even though nothing she could have said or done could have made it *actually* better. But she knew that. That's why it worked.

3. Remain close, even after she moves back to Texas a few years after college. Go there to visit, stay with her and her boyfriend, who also went to school with you. Take a nap on their couch with their dog, even though you usually keep your distance from dogs. Let *her* show *you* around. Eat breakfast tacos and go vintage shopping and take photo booth pictures together that will hang on your fridge forever—a black-and-white strip of the two of you: deadpan, goofy, glam, sweet.

4. When her boyfriend becomes her fiancé, prepare to be a bridesmaid. Write your wedding speech, including the story of how she was nervous to approach the boyfriend-turned-fiancé in college, so you invited him to have coffee with the two of you and then pretended to remember somewhere important you had to be. Talk on the phone about color schemes and disco playlists and promise to tease your hair as big as she wants.

5. When she texts you a few months later that her fiancé has died, ask if you can call, rather than just calling, in case she's not ready to talk. Pick up immediately when she calls in response. Feel the desire to make this not be true for her jolt through your whole body so intensely you want to scream. Remember that there's nothing you can say to make it better. Say only that you're so sorry, so so sorry. That you love her. That you're ready to get on a plane right now. Convince yourself that you can help her through

this. You know the topography of grief; you can point her toward a safe passage.

6. Know that the type of loss she has suffered is especially complicated. But you know something about this particular kind of grief, too. You've never lost a partner, someone you planned to have children with, but you know what it feels like to mourn a person and hate the person who killed them and try to hold in your mind that they are one and the same.

7. Go to Texas again. Sit in her childhood bedroom with her and her mother—all of you on the floor, leaning against the bed and the wall, staying low. Look at the pictures on her walls, relics from before you met her; a version of her that you feel like you know from stories about community theater and her hairdresser grandmother and her childhood dog.

Listen to her explain that she doesn't feel angry at him. Admire her so much for that wisdom and compassion. Say that you do. You do feel angry at him. See a little spark in her mother's eye when you say this.

8. Go with her to the apartment she shared with the fiancé, which she hasn't been able to bring herself to pack up yet. Offer to do it for her, wanting so badly to be useful. But don't push. Don't pick up a single book or dish or article of clothing without a cue from her. See clearly that she's not ready yet, and instead just be near her while she walks from room to room, marveling at her own things as if seeing them for the first

time. When she says maybe she'll just take some crystals with her for now, offer to cleanse them in the sunshine first. Collect all of the crystals from the bookshelves and windowsills, and carry them out into the yard together, talking about how sunlight can burn away just about anything. Sit in the sun together, and hope this is true.

9. Stand waist-deep in the cool water of Barton Springs, squinting in the hot Texas sun, watching as she trails her fingers back and forth, back and forth, across the surface of the water, sending out gentle ripples, talking about how she'll have to start all over again. Not just a new relationship, but a whole new self. "I feel like a newborn baby," she says. Know that she's right. She's a new version of herself now and there's no going back. Grief is a place you can't travel to without being transformed. You eat the seeds and then you become queen of a land you never even wanted to visit.

Feel the slippery algae on the rocks under your feet. Run your hands over the surface of the water, mirroring her, and say, "I can't wait to see what you build."

10. Remember that, of course, there is no map for grief. That her grief is an entirely different country from your own, and the only person who can ever find their way through it is her. Feel silly for thinking you could impose order on something like this. That you could offer her anything more than your presence.

Abandon the idea that you know the way, and instead follow her lead. You are not a guide. You're just keeping her company for part of a journey that will be long and arduous and once in a while even beautiful. But it will be hers alone.

11. When she starts dating again, remind her that she doesn't have to yet, unless she wants to. Worry a little bit that she's rushing herself, but know that if she says she's ready, it won't help her to hear any doubts. Tell her that whatever pace feels right to her, is right. Tell this again to yourself, and believe it.

12. When she meets someone new, like him immediately when she describes how respectful and compassionate and not-threatened he is about her loss. How he understands that it's part of her; that she will always be walking its paths and scaling its cliffs.

13. Go to Texas for a third time. Stand next to her, holding her bouquet, while she and the new man say their vows, and you can see on his face how much he loves her, and you don't believe in god but you thank whatever is out there that your friend has arrived here, in this moment, and that you get to be here to see it. Cry even though you're standing there up in the front and everyone can see you. Remember that conversation in the cool water just a few years earlier, about the brand-new self, the brand-new life. Marvel at how far she has traveled, at all she has built.

It Comes in Waves

Kim Wall's mutilated torso was found eleven days after she boarded a submarine belonging to Danish inventor Peter Madsen, in the summer of 2017. She was a journalist, and he was a source. But in the end, that didn't matter. She had been raped, stabbed, and dismembered.

I followed the story as it unfolded, sick and horrified but unable to look away, my body tensing with each new update. Months after her torso was found, I dreamt that I'd been the last one to see Kim Wall alive before she got on the submarine. In part of the dream, I saw myself on security footage, running, panicked, trying to find someone to tell what I knew. I woke up like coming up from an ice bath, gasping, eyes watering. I woke up still feeling a crushing guilt for letting her get on the submarine in the first place; for not somehow knowing what was going to happen, and stopping it.

I didn't know her in real life, but we'd gone to the same school, knew some people in common. I thought at first that this was why the story of her disappearance and murder caused such a deep ripple in me.

When my cousin Sabina was murdered in 2010, seven years before Kim Wall, the initial shock gave way to frantic thoughts about who could have done it. I called the detectives handling the case to tell them about the dramatic breakup she'd recently been through, to say I didn't know anything for sure but they might want to talk to her ex. She was popular in the club scene in Philadelphia, a budding model whose gigantic smile and fluttering eyelashes surely caused some jealousy. I didn't know all of the social dynamics of her world, but I told the detectives everything I could think of that she'd told me about her life during our regular phone calls. I terrified myself with thoughts of what petty trifle someone had decided was worth such a glowing twenty-year-old's life, running through possible scenarios of advances rebuffed, territories infringed upon, of elaborate grudges and plots. *People have murdered for the most insignificant things,* I thought, wondering if I'd spend the rest of my life saying "over a guy" or "over a modeling job."

I couldn't face the grief yet, the idea that I would never see her again, so instead I focused on what I could do to help, to catch whoever did this; and what I could have done to prevent it from happening in the first place. I was in another state when Sabina was killed, but I wanted so badly to go back and walk her home that night, I almost stretched time. The guilt of the inability to time-travel.

Six months before she died, she posted a photo on Facebook of the two of us as toddlers, me hugging her protectively while she leaned into me. She captioned it "you may have had a big sis, to protect you, but I had my big cus, and that was all I needed!" In the months and then years after her death, I pulled that picture up periodically to torture myself over how it wasn't enough, after all.

Police eventually identified Sabina's killer as an eighteen-year-old kid in her neighborhood, not connected to her in any way. He left her body out in the open to be found in a vacant lot next to her apartment building, where we'd once barbecued, mosquitos biting our legs in the twilight. We were tweens then, eating corn on the cob while our mothers and our uncle and her stepfather (my godfather) grilled burgers and drank beer out of green glass bottles. There were fireflies. Now I can't return to that memory without her naked and bruised body splayed limp at the edge of the image.

Police caught the man that did it because of security camera footage that shows him following her. He denied it, but his DNA was all over her. Evidence that he'd used her body, and that she'd fought him. Later at trial his lawyer claimed she was a sex worker. That she'd had consensual sex with him in an empty lot, right next to her building. They didn't have an explanation for the bruises. For how she ended up dead.

After Kim Wall's torso was found, Madsen claimed she'd been killed in an accident aboard the submarine. All he'd done, he said, was dispose of the body. He had no explanation for the signs of sexual assault. For why he dismembered her.

Not until that dream about the submarine and the familiar feeling of panic, of "It's too late, I should have stopped it," did I understand that my mind had made Kim into Sabina, made Sabina into Kim. That this was why I felt sick every time I went online and saw the face of this woman I had never even met on news stories and fundraisers. It was the same feeling I got seven years earlier when Sabina's story was in the news and an article would pop up with her smiling face and the word MURDER in bold underneath it, and I would close my laptop and need to lie down.

I never read the news stories about Sabina. I couldn't—the images in my mind were already too detailed, too horrific. But I saw the headlines calling her SLAIN WAITRESS and VICTIM, a dehumanization I couldn't stand, but that was almost preferable to the headlines that used her full name, forever associating her name with the monster who shoved her down in the dirt and choked the life out of her, just because he could. Every time someone shared a news story about Sabina, I pictured her fighting for her life and I got the cold tingly feeling all over my body that I'd only ever felt in the moments before fainting.

And now, all these years later, every time someone shared a news update about Kim Wall, I felt that same cold tingly feeling. I pictured screams echoing in the underwater metal of a submarine; imagined how she must have felt when she realized what was happening to her and that there was no escape route. Each update came days, weeks, sometimes months after the last—she was missing, they found the torso, he was arrested. Grief and horror that came in waves, like body parts washing up on shore.

A week after Sabina was killed, my whole family was huddled in my aunt's big creaky house in Philadelphia, the first time all of the aunts and uncles and cousins and our grandmother had been together since Sabina's fifth birthday party, fifteen years earlier. The bittersweet, gutting pain of knowing how pleased she would have been with herself that she'd managed to get us all together. The only one who was always on the outside of our big Irish family's various feuds, she'd been pushing for a reunion for years. Now here we were.

We were in the car, my mother behind the wheel and my aunt—Sabina's mother, my mother's little sister Rachel—in the passenger seat, when Rachel got the call from the coroner with the results of Sabina's autopsy. She listened for a few moments and then, in a shaking voice, she asked, "Was she raped?"

Until that moment, I'd willfully blocked out every detail I could. I didn't want to know if she'd been raped, because in my gut I knew that she had. And I couldn't stand to know it. I knew that once I let even a glimpse of her life ending that way into my mind, I would never escape it. It would come over me in waves and waves for the rest of my life. So, I tried not to know. I'd left the room when detectives came over with updates, I'd turned off the TV when news reports came on, I'd turned newspapers face down on the table.

When Rachel asked the question, I panicked and started yelling "Pull over, pull over!" to my mother as she sped down the highway. I wanted out of the car, wanted to walk in the tall grass along the side of the road and never have to know. But then Rachel screamed, a deep, guttural, violent wail, and it was too late; I knew. The images flooded my mind, and they haven't left.

When we went to the funeral home, I wasn't sure if I wanted to see Sabina's body. More accurately, I knew I didn't want to, but I wasn't sure if I would do it anyway. My mother hadn't let me see my father's body when he died when I was a kid. Didn't want that image in my mind. I fought her decision at the time, but came to be grateful for it. This time, though, as the big-sister figure, I decided that I owed it to Sabina to look at what was left of her. If she had to live through those last moments, I could at least bear witness to their impact.

I took two steps into the room and saw just the top of her head, where she was lying on a raised platform, facing away from the door. I saw her thick black hair, and I turned and ran. Out of the room, out of the building. I ran out into the parking lot and then kept running.

Once, when we were teenagers sharing a bed during a visit, she woke me up in the middle of the night and said I'd been petting her hair in my sleep like she was a cat. We laughed and I apologized, and then I petted her hair a few more times for good measure before we snuggled up and went back to sleep. In the first dream I had about her after she died, we were backstage before a big performance she was nervous about. I understood in the dream that everything would be different after this performance; that I wouldn't see her again. We were sitting on a little couch with her head on my lap, and I was petting her hair, soothing and reassuring her. I woke up with the texture of her hair still tingling on my hands.

I saw that hair on the corpse in the funeral home, and I pictured that hair sticking to tears and sweat on her face. And I ran.

I felt guilt for not being able to even read about what happened to Sabina. Like I felt guilt for not stopping it, like I felt guilt for not being able to force myself to stand in the funeral home and look at her lifeless face. I felt like I should have been able to, like I owed it to her to stand still and let the horror wash over me. But I just couldn't.

For years, part of me was still in that car, my hands over my ears, trying not to know the whole truth of what happened to her.

When Kim Wall disappeared and her face was everywhere, like Sabina's had been, the dam cracked. The defenses I'd built up started to crumble because here was this story that brought back all of those same feelings; the waves of horror and images that wouldn't go away.

I read each update about Kim despite the nausea, even as they seeped into my dreams and brought my panicked guilt and terror sloshing up to the surface. I read the details of what happened to her because I still hadn't been able to force my eyes open to a single news story about Sabina's murder, but this I could almost handle. Because I could read about what happened to Kim without remembering the texture of her hair or the sound of her laugh. Without the horrific images in my mind of what happened to her crowding out happy childhood memories.

I could let the horror wash over me without it sweeping me out to sea.

The Fire Escape

The apartment in the East Village that Leah and I shared in our early twenties was only my bedroom (half of which was taken up by my loft bed and the clothes I hung from its beams), her bedroom (just a little bigger), a kitchen where you could pivot from the stove to the sink to the sliver of counter without picking up your feet, and a bathroom where you could wash your hands while sitting on the toilet. That was it.

That plus the fire escape.

We called it the porch, but the fire escape didn't have the languorous feeling of a covered wraparound, two steps up to a rocking chair. You had to lean against the building or brace against the guardrail to keep from feeling like you might fall five stories down to the street. The fire escape precariously hanging off the side of the building felt just right for us: not so easily approachable as a porch, or something people walking by down below even noticed. We were perched high above the world and its concerns like crows in the treetops.

First, you had to take a big step over the sill so you were half in, half out of the building, straddling the window ledge like a daredevil cowboy; then duck and weave to get the top half of your body out, reaching for the rickety, rust-covered railing. Try not to kick the stove as you pull yourself the rest of the way out. And then sit, right away, so you don't tumble over the rail. And because we never sat out there for small pieces of time, we'd do this climb with full hands—a pack of cigarettes and a lighter in one, or a joint just rolled inside; a full drink in the other. Always a full drink. Sometimes a bottle.

The word "escape" is right there in the name, but it wasn't fire we were running from. Or maybe it was. The everyday fires that sometimes choke you with their smoke, thick and swirling. We were so young, trying to make it on our own: bartending and dating and sometimes in school and then sometimes not. Fighting with our mothers, losing jobs and boyfriends and getting new ones. Whenever Leah or I started to feel like we couldn't breathe, we'd pop into the other's bedroom and say "Fire escape?" and out we'd go.

There was magic to sitting out there alone, too, but really it was about sitting out there together. Literally stepping out of our lives, to drink and smoke and commiserate. Or sometimes just to sit together in silence and look down at the busy street below. Mental and emotional space were as limited in our lives as physical space was in that tiny apartment. Mostly Leah was a blur of long curly red hair and Betsey Johnson perfume flying around the apartment, singing along to Florence and the Machine in her room while she got ready to go out. And I was in and out, rarely at home except to sleep the exhausted sleep of a full-time bar job on top of a full course load. But out there on the fire escape, everything slowed down and expanded. It was a place we could go where we were fully present, together—no TV or music in the background, no putting makeup on or stirring something on the stove or even looking at our phones. Just the rusted metal bars under our asses, the sky feeling as close as the ground.

When Sabina was killed, the fire escape stopped being a place I went and became where I was. I needed an escape not just for a few minutes, but for the whole summer. And so I sat out there, day after day, for hours and hours on end, as one friend after another visited in shifts, bringing booze and cigarettes and food. Not one of them tried to persuade me to come inside, and for that I loved them more than ever. Leah would come out for a bit before she left for work, and then come right back out when she got home.

While everything else felt unsteady with grief, the brick exterior of the building was still solid behind my back, the iron slats leaving deep impressions in my bare legs; a reminder that I was still here, still flesh and blood. From five stories up, the world looked as far away as it felt.

Until finally, one day, I was ready to climb back inside.

Eventually I moved out of that apartment, but Leah stayed, and whenever I came over we'd go right out the window—muscle memory deep in our bodies as we ducked and lunged. Silence falling for a moment as we took in the comfort and familiarity, the safety we felt in this precarious perch, before we launched into an hours-long conversation. We were always extra honest on the fire escape; set apart from the rest of our lives just enough that we could say anything.

When Leah moved out too, a few years later, I went over one last time. It was too cold, the middle of winter, but we managed to squeeze through the window in our big puffy coats and hunker down, leaning into each other against the wind. I'd come prepared with two small glass jars, and we took out our pocketknives and scraped little black and red flakes of painted and corroded iron from the bars of the fire escape into the jars—dirt from sacred ground to take with us as we made new fire escapes for each other out of whatever park or living room we would meet in next.

Before we climbed back in the window for the last time, we took big ceremonial gulps of whiskey, even though we didn't really drink like that anymore. We toasted, "To the fire escape!" knowing what we really meant was "To us! To those years, and how we helped each other survive."

Spell to Mend a Broken Heart

The night was silent except for the rhythmic sloshing of three sets of legs slicing through a gently churning tide as Leah, Liz, and I waded out into the Long Island Sound. We stopped when the cool water reached our thighs, goosebumps forming on our arms as we clasped hands in a circle. The waning moon's reflection glinted on the glassy surface, the sand and pebbles below obscured. Lights in the windows of the neat row of waterside homes broke through the dark night, but we could still see stars as we tilted our faces toward the sky.

Leah's long-term boyfriend had just moved out, a man I thought I might love had abruptly dumped me to get back together with his ex-girlfriend, and someone Liz had feelings for had kissed her in the drunken predawn hours after last call and then pretended it never happened. We met in the emotionally nauseous place of feeling rejected, crushed despite thinking we should be too proud to feel crushed. So we took our shoes off and waded out into the Sound, pouring our heartbreak into the water so we could leave it there. We closed our eyes and said all the things we would've been embarrassed to say out loud in the daylight, letting the water rock us gently back and forth. We released our hurt, declared ourselves washed clean of it.

Carly and Courtney, in the house a hundred yards away, would gladly have joined us in the water. But they were both in committed relationships, and we heartbroken three needed to do this alone. I felt how special our group of five was when they understood this completely, without a hint of feeling left out. We could do things all together during this girls' weekend away—like drive to the farm stand and gather all the berries we could carry, and dance around the living room after dinner until we collapsed on the floor—and we could do things apart, the distinct relationships within the larger group given space to flourish, too.

When Liz, Leah, and I had said all we needed to say, had squeezed each other's hands and breathed the cool night air deep into our chests and let tears roll down our cheeks into the sloshing Sound, we trudged back to the shore, toward the warm lights in the windows. We rinsed the salt water off of our legs with a hose and rejoined Carly and Courtney inside, where they were waiting with cocktails and pie. We spent the rest of the weekend sunbathing, blending margaritas, washing pounds of berries in the deep beach-house sink, and feeling a little bit lighter.

Thirteen years earlier, when I was twelve years old, my father died with nine dollars in his wallet. My mother and I, along with his sister and a handful of his closest friends, traveled to the town of Redway, California, where he had died, to collect his things and have a small memorial service before the larger funeral in San Francisco. Our motel room off the highway, meant to be an anonymous way station, was made overly intimate by the stack of cardboard boxes against one wall, holding all of my father's possessions—his books and art supplies, his worn-thin work boots and leather jacket, and the little stuffed dog I'd mailed him so he wouldn't be lonely out there in the woods. In the canvas backpack that sat atop the stack, my mother found the wallet, thumbing his ID and library card, and the cash. She suggested we spend it on something for me. It would be weird, she said, to just put it in her own wallet—if he'd known this was his last nine dollars, he would've spent it on me.

It was July, and I was tan, my knobby twelve-year-old knees still scraped from running around and being a kid outside in the summer; a life that now felt like a distant past as I drifted, heavy and wordless, behind my mother down the main street of this small hippie town, trying to comprehend a world in which my father would never again send me a postcard about an animal he'd seen that week, or a book he thought I might like, or an art project he hoped I would do with him. He'd written me at least once a week since my parents split up five years earlier, little messages of love and silliness that had sustained me through our distance, now cut off abruptly and forever.

We wandered into a gift shop with tie-dyed shirts hanging in the window and incense burning inside, and I scanned bumper stickers and magnets with pot leaves and dogs in sunglasses advertising "Humboldt, CA," looking for something to be the last present my father would ever buy for me. Near the register, I spotted a small display labeled "Pocket Spells"—palm-sized plastic boxes full of candles and stones and incantations, prepackaged magic promising everything from money to health to protection from bad dreams. I picked up one labeled "Spell to Mend a Broken Heart" and thought,

Couldn't hurt. I handed it to my mother, along with a crystal on a purple-beaded wire, and she hugged me and then paid with the crumpled bills.

At home, after the funeral, I closed my bedroom door, set my marble composition notebook down on the beige carpet, and arranged the box's contents on its cover—a single dried rose petal, a red candle smaller than a birthday candle in a flimsy plastic holder, a piece of red thread, and a paper scroll that reminded me of a diploma I'd once made for my American Girl doll. I unrolled the tiny scroll and followed its instructions—lighting the candle, cutting the thread, and reading aloud a short passage about being free from the heartache of lost love. I changed the words as I read, the spell clearly intended to help someone get over a breakup and not quite applicable to the grief I was feeling. Instead of getting over my lost love, I asked to remember my father forever, but also for the pain of losing him to dull, just a little.

I heard my own thin voice hanging in the air, and my vision blurred with tears as I stared at the tiny flame of the candle that was threatening to tip over on the soft surface of my notebook. I sat cross-legged on the carpet, breathing slowly. I closed my eyes, pictured my father's face—the smile lines around his eyes, the mole on his temple, the curly hair I inherited—and tried to imagine a future where I could think of him without feeling hollowed out.

Afterward, my heart was no less broken, but it had felt good to say out loud what I wanted, what I needed. To feel like I could set myself on a path rather than simply flailing in grief and the already unsteady atmosphere of adolescence. I wanted to feel that again, so I started collecting tools and building an altar: spending my weekly allowance at the flea market and the occult shop downtown on chalices, a dagger, tiny clay bowls for salt and water, candles of various colors, little glass jars of herbs I labeled with masking tape and Sharpie. I collected leaves and rocks and feathers and statuettes of goddesses. I'd always collected small natural objects of fascination—all of my childhood books have leaves between the pages; my pockets were always full of rocks and shells—but now that I was learning the symbolism and sympathetic magic of each stone and flower, I wasn't just collecting, I was building. Building myself, and building a bridge from myself to the world around me.

We had recently moved in with my mother's boyfriend in a converted military base in central California, where I didn't know anyone. My father was gone, and I was living in exile. It was summer when we moved there, right before the funeral, with weeks of vacation before I started seventh grade at a brand-new middle school stretching out vast and shapeless ahead of me. But now I had something to do with my time other than lie in bed staring at the stucco ceiling of my new bedroom and missing my father.

I dove into the study of magic and witchcraft with a hunger and dedication I had never applied to anything before, and one I never quite matched again, not even when I went to graduate school a decade later. I color-coded index cards—green for the magical uses of herbs, yellow for the meanings of stones, red for numerology and color magic, pink for mythology and deities, orange for the uses of tools, purple for moon phases and astrology—and studied them every day. I started with my mother's books—her interest in the occult had been a consistent, unobtrusive presence throughout my childhood: a deck of tarot cards wrapped in silk on her dresser, crystals and herbs offered to ward off nightmares and illness, and this shelf of books I'd never paid attention to but now commandeered without objection from her. When I'd read them all, indexing every bit of tangible information I could find, I started pleading to go to Borders each weekend for one more book. I devoured histories of witchcraft and modern how-to books, encyclopedias of herbs and symbols, folklore and myths from around the world.

When I started building my own Book of Shadows, honing a personal practice from the fragments of everything I was reading, I had no concept of the fact that some spiritual practices were not mine to adopt. So in addition to traditions that were at least adjacent to my heritage—I left offerings to the Celtic goddess Brigid on Imbolc, and compiled my Book of Shadows under the name Lilith, renaming myself after the ferocious she-demon from Jewish myth—I also incorporated things like the burning of white sage (sacred to many Native peoples) into my practice. I placed goddesses from a dozen different traditions next to each other in my personal pantheon, with a belief that various religions and cultures throughout history have been coming up with different faces and names for the same essential concepts—deifying fertility, vengeance, death, abundance, sacrifice, wisdom over and over again in different languages and with some variation but even more repetition. It was this universality that appealed to me—this feeling of rising above the specific trappings of any one tradition in a way that felt both deeply personal and so far beyond me.

I still hold the core belief that drove this approach—that

religions are all more similar than they are different, each born out of a shared and innately human desire to understand the forces that shape our lives and the world around us. That no one tradition gets it all right. But I also have more respect now for the lineage of each practice, and understand that sometimes the best way to respect something is to leave it alone. I no longer burn sage.

When school started, the usual angst I felt at being the new kid was tempered somewhat by the private world I was building. I didn't talk to anyone at school, but in my bedroom, lighting candles and sprinkling herbs in a circle around me, I was cultivating a voice; calling the elements into my circle until it felt like they listened.

The idea of stories about witchcraft as allegories for adolescence has been written about many times, so I won't belabor it here. I'll just say it's no coincidence that so many pop culture depictions of witches focus on teen girls, or that adolescence is the time so many of us first start to explore the occult. When your body is transforming in ways both hideous and mesmerizing, and people start treating you like a danger to yourself and others; when you first suspect that you might be a powerful force right at the same moment everyone around you starts putting new and infuriating limits on your freedom . . . of course you look for an outlet. For a way to stoke the flames inside yourself.

I felt like before I could try casting (my own, non-prepackaged) spells for specific things I wanted, I first had to align myself with the rhythms of the seasons and the moon—to find my way into magic itself. Then maybe I could try to direct it. So on the evening of a full moon, several months into my studies, I locked my bedroom door and turned off the overhead light. My room was in the back of the house, facing a tangle of woods that I liked to stare into, pretending it was a vast, enchanted forest, not just a small patch of green in the middle of a suburban sprawl. The streetlights on the main road didn't reach this rear window, so my altar, a flea-market coffee table in the center of the room, was illuminated only with silver moonlight and candles. I called the four corners one at a time, facing each cardinal direction and sprinkling salt, lighting incense and a red candle, and dipping my fingers into a bowl of water. I sat down at the altar and asked for the light and power and bounty of the full moon to wash over me. I asked to be swept into the rhythm of the moon, and the seasons, and the elements.

I asked to be a witch.

I sat in fervent silence, my cheeks flushed with the effort to be heard. And then, piercing the silence: the distinctive call of an owl.

My mother dreamt of owls when she was pregnant with me, and when I was born with a cleft lip and a fuzzy bald head, I looked like one. She gave me the middle name Tylluan, Welsh for owl; and my artist father drew and sculpted owls, giving them to my mother as talismans of their baby. A particular connection to this bird of prey, companion to my favorite Greek goddess, Athena, had always felt like my birthright. An owl showing up outside my window during this ritual couldn't be a coincidence.

I parted the invisible curtain I'd drawn and stepped out of my circle, rushing to the window. There, in the closest tree, not twenty feet away, was a great horned owl. As I looked out, its wide eyes fixed on mine and it called again, its hooting vibrating down my spine. After the second call, I held my breath and stood perfectly still, this magnificent bird and I staring at each other for a few long seconds before it took off, its massive wingspan propelling it swiftly into the woods and out of sight, illuminated in flight for just a flash by the light of the full moon.

I sat back down at my altar, skin tingling, to give thanks for this visitation and close the ritual. That night, I dreamt vividly of soaring through treetops in pure darkness, able to see sounds and taste the air. Distance surreally collapsed so that what was close was a blur but the smallest movement far off was amplified in high, vibrating contrast. I awoke the next morning feeling powerful and invigorated, the memory of wings in the muscles of my arms.

I got my first period a few days later.

The triple goddess—maiden, mother, and crone; embodied by the moon and reflective of a woman's cycles through the stages of life and through each month—was deeply meaningful to me as an adolescent novice witch. I hesitate to even reference the concept of the divine feminine here, or the connection I felt between my first period, the moon, and my burgeoning power, because of how these ideas have been co-opted by gender essentialists whose perception of what it means to be a woman is so tightly hewn to the physicality of menstruation and childbirth that they think this excludes trans women from both womanhood and witchcraft. But I won't surrender the moon to TERFs, I refuse.

Like all religious and spiritual stories, the connection between menstrual cycles and the moon is an allegory that makes it less scary to be alive. If bleeding once a month makes you part of something celestial and ancient, it's easier to take cramps in stride. But that doesn't mean that's all there is to womanhood. To act like it is misses the point entirely, in fact, of the pagan stories of fertility goddesses and horned gods—the feminine and masculine that we're meant to understand as harmonizing in nature and within ourselves; both sides accessible to any and all of us.

But I wasn't thinking about any of this at twelve years old. All I knew then was that feeling like my body was aligned to cycles on a scale so much larger than myself made the changes in my life seem less terrifying, less permanent. I looked up at the moon and understood that this rocky shore between childhood and the vastness beyond it was not where I would live forever; that this initial swell of grief for my father would recede; that someday all of this would be a memory. And that there was power, not just horror, in change.

In my mid-twenties, I felt once again in flux, cresting the wave of a new cycle. My father had been gone for half of my life—the time I'd known him forever shrinking in comparison to the time I'd spent without him. I'd been not-a-child for as long as I'd been a child, while at the same time feeling like I was only now reaching adulthood. I'd dropped out of high school and then talked my way into college with an essay about how I'd educated myself, and gone on to grad school as if trying to erase any trace of the years I'd spent rejecting the expected path. Now I'd graduated, unsure what I was supposed to do next—continue striving for markers of mainstream success, or retreat to the more comfortable fringes, setting aside the costume of professionalism that still felt ill-fitting, tailored for someone else? And then I'd had my heart broken with the kind of extreme, blindsiding impact that makes you reconsider your own sense of self. I felt, with undeniable clarity, that it was time to decide who I was going to be.

So I took my tarot cards out of their silk pouch for the first time in years. Brought a few of my favorite tools out of the box in the back of my closet—my chalices and bowls and a snakeskin-handled dagger my mother had brought back for me from Morocco. These things felt like reminders that I was capable of building whatever version of myself I chose. I pulled the Magician card over and over and over again—change, the ability to manifest, potential waiting to be directed. The cards being coy, telling me that yes, I was at a turning point and I had the power to create whatever I wanted . . . but refusing to tell me what I should want.

I started reading tarot for friends, late at night. I pulled a card for Courtney after a night out at the bar, the two of us cross-legged on my bed, drinking tall glasses of ice-cold water, my orange tabby cat watching us through half-closed eyes, purring. Courtney listed several different paths forward in her life, each mutually exclusive from the rest, and asked for a guiding principle by which to choose.

I did a full spread—on the floor, with wine and candles—for Carly when she was deciding whether to move home to Texas. My heart fell when she pulled the Chariot: I didn't want her to go, but it was clear that she would. It felt like the cards were telling me to accept this as much as they were telling her what she already knew.

When Leah's boyfriend moved out, I came over with crystals and wine, to cleanse the space and reconsecrate it as hers alone. We opened all the windows and burned incense and blasted music and sat in every corner of the apartment.

Liz and I didn't light candles or set up an altar, but every conversation we had about the lives we were building had the feeling of an incantation. Every debaucherous night out a sacred bacchanal.

I could see that we were all going through this churn of one life transforming into another, and it made me notice the moon all over again. Reminded me that life is made up of cycles.

As the summer solstice approached, the five of us agreed that we deserved a long weekend away. We were all tired and raw from the exertion of building adult lives, and Carly was leaving at the end of the summer (she had officially decided). And so: a girls' trip to Long Island, with nothing to do but sleep in and get sunburns and cook for each other, and live as if we had all the time in the world to be exactly who we were, right then, before becoming our next selves.

I don't remember whose idea it was for me, Leah, and Liz to wade out into the water. Only that the three of us had commiserated over our various romantic woes until the energy of everything we were feeling and saying took its own shape. Someone must have spoken the idea aloud at some point, but it feels like it carried us along on its own current, out into the cool water.

My mother and I moved back home to New York the summer before I started high school. On the first day I asked a girl in my homeroom with icy blue eyes if her name, Raiona, was connected to the Celtic goddess Rhiannon. She said it wasn't, but she was intrigued. I told her what I knew about Rhiannon, a figure from Welsh mythology always depicted riding a horse, variously associated with the moon, rebirth, travel, and creative inspiration. Our friendship started in that moment, built on myths. I read her tarot cards in the schoolyard, and before long we'd decided I would teach her what I knew about magic.

I had so far been a solitary witch, but I thrilled at the idea of a coven—even one with only two members. I'd always wanted a sister; a bond deeper than friendship, someone to be so attuned to that we could communicate without speaking. I imagined the heights we could reach by combining our power, remembering *The Craft* and *Practical Magic* and every movie I'd ever seen about witches tapping into something larger together than they ever could have on their own. The idea of sharing what I'd learned made it feel more real, like all of my studying had been in preparation for whatever Raiona and I were about to embark on together.

I was also excited to be in charge. I'd always wanted a sister, yes, but a younger sister, specifically. Raiona was actually one week older than me, but still, I was in the position of imparting knowledge—able to think of myself as a high priestess sharing secrets rather than a novice seeking them. I'd always been a bossy kid on the playground, teaching my friends the rules of games I was making up as we went along, so I stepped into the leader role easily in our coven of two.

I gave Raiona assigned readings and a list of tools she was to collect. I helped her pick out a silver pentagram necklace with a moonstone in the center, similar to the one I wore every day. She was to keep it with her tools to absorb their magic, I explained, but not wear it until we completed her teaching and held an initiation ceremony.

Our friendship grew in other areas too—soon we were two out of a big group of downtown misfit kids who skipped class and went to shows and got drunk in the park. We dropped acid in Central Park and walked all the way back to the East Village, clinging to each other in giddy terror as we navigated the fun house of Times Square; we stayed out all night making up songs and stories and plans for the future. I gave her a blue-and-white Pendleton shirt that had been my father's—the first thing of his I ever gave away—because blue was her color, matching her eyes and her cobalt-dyed hair, and because sharing my most meaningful possessions was the only way I could think of to express the depth of our bond.

On the solstices and full moons, I carted a red plaid vintage bowling bag full of my tools on the subway from my apartment on the Lower East Side to hers in the Bronx—silver chalices, a small wrought iron cauldron, a clay pentagram dish, little velvet bags full of feathers and stones and candles and bundles of herbs. We dressed in our flowiest clothes and embarked deep into Pelham Bay Park—as far out into nature as two New York City teens could get.

The ritual started as soon as we entered the park, quiet coming over us as we trudged deeper into the urban woods. One time, as we followed the twisting path toward the Bay, we saw a bundle of sticks and some melted wax on a tree stump and thrilled at the idea that we were not the only ones doing magic there.

We finally reached the water, frothy with pollution, and set up our altar on a fallen log, laying everything out just so: The white candle and the dagger in the south for fire, the little bronze censer and feathers in the east for air, quartz and a bowl of salt in the north for earth, my flea-market chalices in the west for water.

On these nights in the park, we did spells for protection, love, money, creative inspiration—sometimes working together toward a common aim and sometimes each making our own requests and offerings after building the circle together. Some worked and others didn't. I once found twenty dollars on the street less than an hour after a money spell, but was never able to replicate that result. And a boy I liked kissed me out of nowhere a few days after I visualized his face while holding a rose petal in my mouth. But those moments of fruition, tantalizing as they were, ultimately mattered less than the feeling of sitting in the magic circle together. In our daily lives, we fought with our parents and got caught up in petty drama with friends; we worked shitty jobs and watched our neighborhoods gentrify and wondered if we'd be able to stay in the city we loved when we had to start paying rent in a few short years; we fretted about how quickly time was moving, preemptively nostalgic for these days when we could wander into Tompkins and always find someone we knew there, waiting. But in the circle, all of that faded away. The constant motion of life slowed to a resonant hum radiating through our bodies, up to the sky and deep into the ground.

After a year or so, when Raiona suggested it was time for her initiation ceremony, I felt uneasy. It wasn't something I fully understood or could articulate, but I think a part of me knew I had messed up: I'd turned Raiona's magic into something I could bestow upon her, taken the experience of building from her and turned it into one of receiving, just because I'd gotten a two-year head start reading books and collecting knick-knacks.

When she asked, I didn't know how to explain my mistake, that it wasn't my place to declare her a witch, only she could do that. Instead, I said, "I don't think you're ready yet"—because teenagers are jerks, and because I didn't fully understand where my hesitation was coming from. She accepted my refusal, but afterward something shifted. We started forgetting or not feeling up to big rituals every full moon, saying we'd do something big for the next solstice and then not. We never said we were going to stop doing rituals together, but slowly, we did.

Looking back, I see how easily this anticlimax could have ended our friendship, but instead we let this element fade away and focused on others instead. We'd been talking about taking a big trip to Europe together, and we started focusing all of our drive, attention to detail, and knack for manifestation toward that goal instead—making lists of cities and hostels and train routes instead of herbs and goddesses and incantations. We stepped casually down from our uneven heights and walked forward together on level ground.

After months of disuse, I packed up my tools in a box and put them on a high shelf in my closet. I stopped wearing my pentagram necklace. I still paid attention to the seasons and the moon, but the outward practice of witchcraft felt like just one more part of my childhood to leave behind, one of many skins I was shedding on the way to adulthood. It was time to focus on what I wanted to build in the material world—college applications and rent and a whole new self-image. After years as a degenerate kid in handmade clothes casting spells in city parks, I became a polished, ambitious young adult. It did occur to me that perhaps I was simply casting my most successful glamour spell yet, projecting the version of myself I wanted the world to see.

Raiona and I laughed together, a decade later, about how we'd both approached witchcraft like a class we could get A's in. We were lying on a blanket in Prospect Park, slipping so easily back into our old habit of whiling away an entire day in a park, not bothering to keep track of the time. I mentioned that I'd been thinking about the initiation ceremony we never had, realizing it had never been my place to bestow anything on her. "Sorry I was such a brat," I said. She laughed and said she had been as eager for the teacher-student dynamic as I was—it gave her something clear to work toward, as if she could get a gold star and an official Witch Certificate at the end. She said she'd kept her pentagram necklace in its velvet pouch for years, never wearing it, until eventually she realized she had "earned it" a long time ago and put it on. I was so pleased to hear she'd made that decision on her own, and I considered dusting mine off, too.

It was around this time that my chalices—corroded from the polluted waters of Pelham Bay—made their way out of the closet and onto the top of my bookshelf; that I brought my tarot cards out and pulled the Magician so often it started to feel like a taunt. After the fallow period of my late teens and early twenties, my slow return to magic took a new, much more understated form. I started acknowledging the solstices with something small like a cupcake or a nice glass of wine, making a point to go outside and look up at the full moon for a few quiet moments, and intentionally timing efforts to either gain or release things in my life with the moon's waxing and waning. I found I could access the expansive, buzzing calm of ritual by simply closing my eyes and focusing—I didn't need to trek into the woods carrying a bowling bag full of tools.

I was reminded often of the tarot cards on my mother's dresser, the books she never pushed on me but lent readily when I asked for them. There was power in subtlety, I was learning; in the simplicity of grounded self-assuredness that doesn't need to announce itself.

As Liz, Leah, and I emerged from the Sound, legs tingling when they met the warm summer night air after being submerged in cold, I remembered the first spell I had ever done, almost exactly half of my lifetime earlier. Here was another spell to mend a broken heart, but this time an authentic, organic spell, based purely on instinct. It didn't come in a box, prepackaged or prescribed by anyone else, and it required no trappings—not even a candle. And there was no hierarchy: no priestess and no disciples. Our hands clasped together, on even footing, created a more powerful circle than any drawn in smoke or salt.

Our broken hearts weren't immediately mended when we left the water, dripping onto the grass. But we did all heal in one way or another soon enough. The man I'd been heartbroken over came to the bar where I worked and apologized, saying he'd made a huge mistake, and before long we were back together. I remembered early in our rekindling that I'd chosen my wording very carefully that night in the water: I had asked to be free of the pain of our breakup, to move on from my heartache. Not necessarily to move on from *him*.

When we eventually got married, the same four women from that weekend stood next to me during the ceremony in coordinated jewel-toned dresses. There was no maid of honor, no one of the four singled out as more important to me than the rest. To mark the occasion, I bought for the five of us a set of small antique pewter goblets to use as candleholders. We were flung far apart now, living our adult lives in New York, Seattle, San Francisco, and Austin. With these candles, I proposed, we could stay connected through something more tangible than phone calls.

Now we're all once again in a period of transition—another wedding, a baby, career changes and illnesses. And with each big moment in any of our lives, a text thread of five photos of five lit candles in matching holders, in five different bedrooms spread across thousands of miles. A quiet spell that reminds me that what I most wanted from magic when I was twelve years old, alone and grieving, was to feel like I was part of something vast and powerful.

The Rose Tattoo

A photograph: Sabina and me at my wedding, hugging each other tight, faces pressed together, like so many photos of us taken since we were little. My blond curls in an updo with baby's breath pinned into it; her straight black hair blown out, swept off of her wide cheekbones, hot pink eye shadow emphasizing the vibrant brightness of her smile.

A photograph: The two of us laughing at the reception, candid. We're under the hanging lights, glowing round and warm—her mouth is open and her nose wrinkled, body bent forward, toward me. I'm leaning back a little, my hand on my chest, trying to catch my breath; trying not to laugh so hard my mascara runs. Both of our mothers are visible in the background, two sisters standing together at the bar.

A photograph: Sabina and my brand-new husband, Soomin, talking to each other, leaning against a wall in the packed venue. Her smiling up at him, hands clasped in front of her, shoulders slightly raised—the sweet girly pose she always struck when trying to make a good impression. Him holding a Scotch on the rocks, face contorted with speech—cracking a joke. His hand is on the wall by her shoulder; the toe of one of her silver pumps lifted off the floor, mid-fidget.

None of these photographs exist.

Sabina was murdered five years before I married a man who never met her, who knew her only as a sad story from my past, the reason I won't watch some movies, a framed photo by my bed (the two of us at my fifth birthday party, hugging each other tight, faces pressed together).

But I can see them so clearly, can imagine her moving forward through life with me rather than frozen forever at twenty years old.

Rose tattoos are cliché. An overdone motif.

But Sabina's middle name was Rose, and when she died, my aversion to cliché became irrelevant. She died in June, when roses were in full bloom—seemingly more of them than ever before, bursting urgently out of yards and gardens, gorgeous and excruciating. I needed one that I could keep, frozen in full bloom *and* moving forward through life with me.

As the needle buzzed back and forth, back and forth, shading red petals along the tender edge of my shoulder blade, I thought, *I would live with this pain every day for the rest of my life if it would bring her back*. Then I questioned whether I really meant it, whether I could live with this bruising, scraping pain forever. It seemed impossible. But then, so did living with the bruising, scraping pain of her absence.

In the months before my wedding, four of my closest friends and I discussed hair, makeup. We texted photos of shoes and dresses back and forth. I booked an appointment for us all to get our nails done together, and an image flashed in my mind: Sabina at the nail salon with us, laughing and bonding with these friends of mine who never met her.

Instead, I had the back of my dress altered, lowered two inches so it would display the big red rose, the green stem curling along my spine into the letter *S*. I added one more appointment to the long list of haircut, teeth whitening, facial: a tattoo touch-up so the rose would be at its most vibrant. As I felt the familiar sting of the gun on that same sensitive bone-edge spot, I closed my eyes and imagined that this was the two of us, getting ready together. This was Sabina's hair appointment, her manicure. She was next to me in a chair in a salon, and this pain was a leg wax or maybe bleach on my scalp. It would pass in a moment, and then we'd go to lunch together.

A photograph that does exist: Me and Soomin at our wedding reception, my back to the camera, face in profile. Standing in the middle of the crowded room, under the hanging lights, glowing round and warm.

On my back, framed perfectly by the white silk of my dress: Sabina's rose.

Mutual Mothering

Liz and I spent our early twenties together, singing along to jukeboxes and fighting random men over the pool table and yelling "Shots!," scampering from one bar to the next like mischievous sprites finding and causing trouble. We stumbled along East Village streets supporting each other's weight and laughing, letting people get out of our way. Sometimes we'd both wear tight clothes and lots of eye makeup and we'd revel in all of the eyes that followed us as we walked across the room; other nights we'd both show up in loose jeans, hair greasy, sitting in a corner sipping whiskey and arguing about books, shooing away any man who dared interrupt.

When I was bartending, Liz would come hang out for hours. When I wasn't helping customers, I leaned on the bar and talked to her like it was any other night out. When I stepped away, I watched in my periphery as guys approached her and she made quick decisions about whether to be smiley and sweet, or shoot them down hard and fast. Her slender bronze shoulders rounded over her drink or a book, shiny black hair falling over her heart-shaped face, they threw themselves at her like moths against a porch light. One time a man asked what the poem tattooed on her arm in Spanish meant, reaching out to touch the lines of script, a classic boorish move

I've pulled my own tattooed arm away from with disgust a hundred times. Liz set her bottle of Bud down, turned her head sharply, raptor-like, toward the man, and replied, "It says 'Don't fucking touch me.' "

We weren't all snark and bombast, though. My favorite memories of our nights out are the cab rides home, huddled together in the backseat, speeding through empty streets. I can still feel the gentle jostling of the cab barreling up First Avenue, hear the echoing quiet of the enclosed space after hours in a loud bar, smell the whiskey breath and cigarette smoke. I've never been in a confessional booth, but I imagine it would feel something like those cab rides—holy and quiet, safely contained. Knowing you could say anything, absolutely anything, and the person in there with you would keep your secrets. This was where we tended to each other's hurt feelings and insecurities with the tenderness of mothers putting Band-Aids on scraped knees, comforting and absolving each other.

Almost a decade after the last of those late nights, Liz comes over and we sit on either end of my couch, sipping white wine with ice cubes. My feet, in wool socks, are on the cushion between us, hers are on the coffee table, and she's holding a velvet throw pillow on her lap. A mellow playlist is on low, the room lit by lamplight. It feels so still and calm, like the air in the room is vibrating at a lower frequency than it did back then. We laugh trying to describe that time to each other, rolling our heads around as we attempt to recapture the kinetic feeling—everything in motion, and so loud, a constant fever pitch. It feels so far away now.

I tell her I've been thinking of that period of our relationship in terms of mothering, that I feel like we mothered each other through a second adolescence, and ask if that feels true to her.

"Oh yeah," she says, "I remember feeling like your door was always open, and it was a place of safety, which I think is why it was so fun to act out. The basis of our relationship was always caregiving, so I never felt unsafe even when we were being really wild."

I hadn't quite made the connection that it was the safety and comfort of our relationship that made the raucousness possible, but it feels exactly right when she says it.

This form of care, the idea that friends can mother each other, was a mode of loving I learned when my fellow park kids and I took care of each other as teenagers—leaning on each other in the absence of stable home lives; drying each other's tears, fighting each other's battles.

The first time I met Heather, I was on ecstasy in Tompkins Square Park. I was sitting in the grass with Raiona and Rakhel, trying and failing to roll myself a cigarette. My hands were too sweaty and shaky, and I kept getting distracted. I had been trying for twenty minutes when this chick Heather who I'd seen around a few times came and plopped down in the grass next to me, lifted her giant sunglasses, and asked, "Want me to roll you one?"

She was backlit by the afternoon sun in a way that made her wavy dark brown hair glow gold and red. I was stunned at first by this benevolent apparition, handing her my mangled rolling paper without a word. She sat there, chatting, rolling one cigarette after another, and lighting one for herself. Eventually she got up to leave, but not before refilling the gallon of water we were sharing at the fountain and telling us all to have a beautiful day. And then she was gone, and I wondered for a moment if she'd been real.

The tender generosity of this first interaction colored the rest of our friendship—I never forgot that when we were complete strangers, Heather had abandoned whatever she'd been on her way to do to sit in the grass and roll me an afternoon's worth of cigarettes. It was a small gesture, but it felt significant—and not only because I was on a drug that makes everything feel significant. It set the tone of our relationship as one in which we would do whatever we could to make each other feel cared for. Maybe that's the heart of what I'm writing about here: care. Not just to care *about* someone but to care *for* them. To take care of.

I returned that care whenever I could for Heather. She usually went home earlier than I did—she had a parent who kept track of her comings and goings and couldn't get away with staying out until sunrise every night, so she said her goodbyes around midnight. Sometimes she took the M15 bus down Second Avenue, but sometimes, if we were in the middle of a good conversation, or if she was a little too drunk and needed to walk it off before she got home, I walked her from the East Village to her father's apartment near the South Street Seaport, about two miles through the bar crowds of the Lower East Side and then the emptier streets of Chinatown. I never wanted her to make the walk alone; it didn't seem safe. I walked her up to the door of her building, and then made the same walk through the same streets by myself. To prioritize another person's safety and well-being and comfort; maybe this is what I mean by mothering.

Right at the height of our wildness, Liz and I both got rejected by guys we really, actually liked—the tables unfairly turned. We wallowed together for a whole summer, with such abandon that it almost felt good to feel so shattered. We didn't just sit and feel bad for ourselves, we swam through our heartbreak, kicking and thrashing, breathing it in and coughing it back up again. We sang along to Hole at the top of our lungs even when the bar wasn't that crowded, and it was early, and nobody else was being rowdy yet. We cried right there at our table at the bar, and out front smoking cigarettes, and on street corners. I used to cry a lot as a teenager, but then somewhere along the way I zipped my emotions back up inside myself like a tight dress. With Liz they came pouring back out.

Sitting on my couch, I refill our wineglasses and ask Liz what she remembers about this summer in particular, and there's one thing she remembers differently than I do: I remember so many tears, everywhere, but for her, one specific time that I cried stands out as unusual.

"There was this one night you were bartending, and I remember you grabbed my wrist and dragged me into the bathroom and you started crying," she says. "And you were so upset because Soomin had just come into the bar. Seeing you cry was really disarming, like when you see a parent cry. I was like, 'I can't believe she's showing this much emotion over a guy.' It was astonishing, but then I knew you really loved him, and that you felt a safety in our dynamic to express how much you were hurting."

I laugh when she says this, because she knew I loved him before I did, and I always remember her as the first one to say it out loud. I felt like I should be too proud to ever speak to Soomin again after he dumped me, but I always hoped to see him at the bar, even if it made me cry, just to be in the same room and scrupulously ignore him. Liz and I were out one night when he texted me, and I blurted out, "I think if Soomin apologized, I might give him another chance." I was embarrassed by this confession—an admission that I was guilty of weakness. I expected Liz to admonish me to be strong, to say I was better off without him. Instead, she looked at me with so much tenderness and said, "Of course you would. You love him." It wasn't dismissive, the way she said it—it was generous, a statement of fact that was also permission. In that moment, she was a mother to me, encouraging me to grow into the next version of myself.

When Soomin and I got married a few years later, I made it through the whole ceremony and most of the reception without shedding a tear—until Liz got up and made a beautiful speech that made me cry like a baby.

To be clear, I understand that mutual mothering between friends is not the same as the full-soul commitment of literally mothering a child. What I'm suggesting is a distinction between the state of being a mother and the act of mothering. In separating the two, I'm not trying to diminish the demanding, grueling, joyful work of being a mother—merely to recognize that being a mother is not the only situation in which one might have the opportunity to mother. To nurture and care for another person, to provide them with tenderness and emotional shelter from a world that mostly doesn't give a shit about them. To love so fiercely and with such unrestraint that the recipient of that love feels sustained by it, and never feels fully alone in the world. This is what my closest friends give to me, and what I try to give to them.

But I know that this is only one slice of what it means to be a mother. I know because in addition to this mothering between friends, I have played a small part in the literal mothering of a child. When I was sixteen and had recently moved out of my mother's apartment into a place in Brooklyn with three friends, my friend Jael had a new baby and nowhere to go, so I invited her to live with me. It didn't even occur to me to just wish her the best and move on with my life when I had a bedroom that could technically fit another teenager and a baby in it.

When they moved in, I helped with the baby, Riley—changing her diapers, feeding and burping her, reading her stories and singing to her until she fell asleep, shushing the roommates and whatever friends were over so they wouldn't wake her, opening the living room windows so pot smoke wouldn't drift down the hall toward her crib.

I remember my first day alone in the apartment with Riley so clearly. When she cried, I stared down at her in her crib, understanding with a new solemnity that I was the only one, in that moment, who could give her what she needed. I laid one hand on her belly, taut and round under her cotton onesie. She was so small, her compact little body dense with need, expressing that need as best she could—with one piercing wail after another.

I was still two years away from legal adulthood—it was only by the luck of a greedy landlord that I, along with my equally immature friends, had been allowed to rent this apartment. Sometimes it felt like we were going to be busted at any moment, like it must be illegal for us to be living here like this, playing at real life. Like tomorrow, or the next day, someone's parents would come home from vacation and we'd all have to leave. But day after day, we came home from our various off-the-books jobs to this place we paid for in cash, and there were no adults. Or we were the adults, sort of. It had already felt surreal, tenuous, and now there was a baby here too, somehow. And with everyone else at work, it was up to me to keep her alive.

"Okay, okay," I said to her, in my best impression of a grown woman, as I scooped her up and awkwardly positioned her in my arms.

I'd fed her and changed her already, and felt cocky when she'd stopped crying after each of those ministrations. But now she was crying again, and I'd reached the end of the list of things I knew a baby might cry about. I didn't know what else to do, so I just held her and paced up and down the long hallway, swaying and bouncing and rubbing her back, talking to her about whatever popped into my head—books I'd read and people I'd met and how very loud she was screaming—for what felt like an hour. It could have been ten minutes. I have no idea. We were outside of time, the two of us, existing only in the echo of her cries and the vastness of my incapacity to stem them.

I felt like I was watching us in a movie. I'd seen this scene so many times before: The young mother, harried, desperate, her hair in disarray and her clothes dirty, pleading with a baby to just please stop crying, *Please!* But even as I felt like I was reading from a script, like *All right, this is where I start crying too because I'm so overwhelmed*—it didn't make it any less strenuous. The noise, the sheer volume, of a baby's unrelenting cries really does get to you. I could feel each cry reverberating through the bones of my skull. But more than the noise, it was the strain I imagined it was putting on her that distressed me—surely she must be getting dehydrated, her throat sore. I thought about how I got a headache if I cried too hard for too long, and wondered if that happened to babies too.

Real worry started to pierce my affected practicality. *What if something is seriously wrong? Should I take her to the ER? Should I call Jael at work?* While all of this was running through my mind, I kept bouncing her, shushing and cooing. I started rhythmically patting her back and swaying back and forth as I tried to think of what else she might want, when she made a hiccupping sound and then I felt a warm, wet stream of spit-up slide down my back. And she stopped crying. I held her away from me and looked at her face, still red, tears hanging off of her delicate little lashes, spit-up on her chin—smiling. I laughed, so relieved I didn't even mind my shirt sticking to my back with partially digested formula.

I wiped her chin and changed my shirt, and kept bouncing her until eventually her cheek rested against my shoulder, and she was quiet, heavy with sleep.

"Yeah, you're okay," I whispered into the top of her head. "You're okay. We've got this."

The love I felt for Riley—and that I feel for her still, watching her grow up and past the age I was when she came into my life—is different from the love I feel for my friends. But it's also because I've felt that sharpness of devotion—the certainty that I would do absolutely anything to keep her safe and happy, that my discomfort was meaningless in the face of her need—that I'm able to recognize threads of those same feelings in my love for my friends.

I've wanted to write about the ways in which my friends and I have mothered each other for a long time, but it didn't occur to me until I started actually making notes for this essay how obvious it is that these thoughts would bubble up with a new urgency while I was in the process of deciding whether I wanted to mother a child of my own.

When we were looking at the apartment we live in now—an apartment that we knew, if we took it, we'd live in for several years—Soomin commented about the small second bedroom that was to be my office, "This would totally work as a kid's room, too, eventually."

In that moment, I didn't picture our adorable baby sleeping in that room, the walls painted a pale and soothing color, a rocking chair in the corner. . . . I only pictured my desk disappearing, my laptop balancing precariously on my nightstand, my notebooks strewn about the apartment—or worse, unused on a shelf. I didn't feel expansiveness in that future, I felt only fear. A fight-or-flight response to the idea of my career, the writing life I've worked so hard to build—starting with the room that represented these things—being taken from me. I didn't know how to articulate the freight train of panic careening through my body, so I just nodded and agreed, and we moved on to assessing closet space and shower pressure.

Over the next few weeks, I obsessed over the symbolism of my office being turned into a kid's room. It felt intolerably literal. It was in those weeks that I first started to suspect maybe it wasn't only that I didn't want a baby *yet*. I'd always felt like I wasn't ready *yet,* but at some point in the future I would be. We would be ready, and we'd do it. Children had always been part of the future Soomin and I planned together—ever since an early date when he half-jokingly suggested we buy a Nirvana onesie we saw in a store window and hold on to it "for later," and that was how I knew he was as serious about me as I was about him. Conversations about how we plan to raise our kids—whether we'll take them to synagogue on the high holidays, whether we'd push them to keep at a musical instrument or a sport they've lost interest in, the relative value of summer camp, names we love and hate—have flowed alongside our daily life like an unobtrusive but ever-present stream. A big part of why I wanted to marry him was what a good father I imagined he'd be. Someday.

But now all of a sudden "someday" was imminent—unfolding in the very apartment we were about to move into, in the current era of our lives—and I still didn't feel ready. Instead, I felt full of dread, like the window on my life was closing as I rapidly approached the age at which a pregnancy would be considered "geriatric." Everything I'd built—the sweet, steady life Soomin and I have made together; a fulfilling career that took years of scraping and hustling to build, where I no longer have to tend bar to support my writing but actually get to read and write all day and get paid for it; a home that feels like a sanctuary—was about to be snatched away.

When I finally told Soomin I hadn't stopped thinking about that comment, that I'd been frantic with worry, feeling backed into a corner, he was immediately apologetic.

"Oh, sweetie," he said, in the tender tone that slows my heart rate every time. (Yes, sometimes I feel mothered by my husband, too.) We were lying on a blanket in Central Park, talking about our imminent move into the apartment with the office/nursery, feet in the grass. I had an arm thrown over my eyes—shielded from the sun and from my confession. He reassured me in his confident, practical way that of course my career would always be a priority. We could get a bigger place if we needed to, or if a separate office for me ended up making more sense, it would be a shared expense. I started to cry as he promised he didn't expect me to give up all of the space that was currently mine in our lives for a baby. I knew he didn't expect that, but hearing him say it and feeling the tears roll toward my ears, I understood how deeply I'd internalized the idea that it would be inevitable, whether he asked me to or not. A given, like the second bedroom belonging to the child and not the mother.

Whether I wanted to be a mother felt like something I should talk to my own mother about, but we hadn't spoken in over a year, since the publication of my first book. I wrote a memoir about my father, but inevitably it became partly about my mother, too. Our family was just the three of us—I couldn't write about my relationship with him separate from her. And I couldn't write about grieving his death without writing about what it was like when she became my only parent.

My mother was a wonderful mother when I was little. She was attentive to the small concerns that felt huge—like how a plate of buttery noodles could be utterly ruined by a dusting of chopped parsley, or how essential it was that I got to press the elevator button. When I couldn't sleep, she would gently massage my temples and tell me to imagine clouds floating across a blue sky. When I said I didn't like it when strangers touched my curls, my mother didn't reassure me that they were just being friendly—she helped me practice saying "You have no right to touch me!" until I could say it with confidence. She taught me about magic and assured me that of course fairy tales were real, and I could be both the princess and the witch if I wanted; and the hunter, too. She made all of my Halloween costumes from scratch, and taught me how to sew dresses for my dolls with the scraps. She let me dye my hair purple when I was eleven and stared blankly at other adults who questioned whether that was such a good idea. "It's her body," she said with a finality that ended the conversation every time. She was tenderly attentive and fiercely protective at once, and this, I think, is what it means to mother.

But then my father died and I stopped going to school and started spending my time getting drunk and high in the park instead, and my mother didn't know how to handle me. I pushed her away, like all teenagers do, but she actually let me. "You were impossible," she told me years later.

"You should have kept trying anyway" was all I could say back.

It was in writing about my grief over my father that I first articulated the dysfunction in my relationship with my mother, and my feeling of being emotionally abandoned by her when I became a "difficult" teenager. I'd cauterized the part of me that needed her then, and never felt fully emotionally connected to her since—looking for mothers elsewhere instead. The process of writing all of this peeled away some layers of scar tissue, and in some ways made us closer than we'd ever been. The project gave us a safe forum in which to have real, hard, tearful conversations about what was between us, and what was not.

In the lead-up to publication, I told her things I'd never told her before—including just how angry I still was at her—

trying to prepare her for what was in the book. I told her also that the book represented years of what my emotions had been, but that didn't mean I still felt everything I wrote about feeling. She said she understood, and I felt like we were almost ready to move into a new chapter of our relationship. Like maybe I'd purged the last of my teen anguish once and for all, and soon I could be one of those grown women who calls her mother her best friend. I've always thought it must be so nice to be one of those women, like they never had to fully leave the safety of early childhood.

Even as I wrote about how hurt I was, I felt like I was writing my way back to her. I wrote just past the point where I'd actually arrived in the process of forgiving her, like opening a door for us to step through together.

That's not how she saw it. She read my descriptions of how I felt toward her as a teenager, grieving and angry and feeling so very alone, and called the book "venomous" and "full of hate."

"Didn't you see the love?" I asked, but it was too late. In writing into the crater between us, I'd blown it open, deeper and wider, until it felt impassable.

I don't want to write about my mother anymore. You'd think I would have learned my lesson. But how can I write about what mothering means to me without writing about how I've been mothered, and how I haven't?

These days I feel most mothered by Leah. Leah and I met when she was dating someone I'd previously dated, but that only defined our relationship for about an hour. We laughed for the duration of one drink about this guy having a type—

both of us loud, opinionated Jewish women with big curly hair, nose rings, a preference for Irish whiskey on the rocks, and a tendency to wear all black. But he became irrelevant as we sat next to each other at a bar and that particular excitement buzzed between us, when you know while it's happening that you're connecting with someone. We ended up at another bar much later that night, and I remember blurry flashes of dancing with her to Joan Jett after several whiskeys and saying something drunkenly earnest like "You're great, we should be friends!" I only remember saying this because I remember her response: "Oh girl, we *are* friends!"

Not long after that, the boutique I was working at closed unexpectedly, and Leah helped me get a job waiting tables at the restaurant where she worked. And not long after *that,* my roommate moved out without giving me any notice, and Leah invited me to live with her. In those two moves, she was already mothering me—reaching out to catch me, telling me it would be okay and *Just come over here, don't worry, I've got you.* I was so used to being completely on my own when it came to practical things like work and housing, the idea that a friend would or even could look out for me like that made me devoted to her.

We lived together for four years, during which we forged for each other and ourselves a new sense of home. I wandered into her bedroom often, where we shared the little triumphs and pains of our lives while she got ready for work. And when I became too laser-focused on school and then the beginnings of the project that would become my first book, Leah interrupted with a knock at my door at just the right intervals, inviting me to take a cigarette break with her on our fire escape and come back into the three-dimensional world for a few minutes. We lived our separate lives, but whenever we crossed paths in the kitchen of our comically small East Village apartment, we fed each other some of whatever we were cooking.

When my cousin Sabina was killed, Leah came home shortly after I got the news, and found me curled up on my bedroom floor, sobbing and dry heaving. She asked what had happened, and when I told her, she turned around and left again immediately. At first I thought she didn't know how to handle it, which I could understand. I didn't either. I was howling like an injured animal, contorted on the ground; probably a disturbing sight. But a few minutes later she came back in with a dozen roses and a liter of Jameson and sat right down on the floor with me, where I cried into her lap.

It was while I was living with Leah that Liz and I first got close, and it wasn't long before the three of us were spending long nights together on the fire escape, drinking whiskey out of mason jars, chain-smoking, and reveling in being perched above the world, young and free and loved.

A family friend, a photography professor, texted one day saying that a student of hers was doing a project on chosen families, and she'd thought of me and my friends as potential subjects. I felt proud that she'd recognized the special bond we had, and told her we were in. We asked to be photographed on the fire escape, the clear representative location of our time as a trio.

When the photography student arrived, she asked jokingly who were the moms and who was the baby. Without missing a beat we all said, "We're all both."

I have a framed print of one of the pictures from that day hanging in my office—this one from the roof. Leah and I are standing, my head on her shoulder and her cheek on my head, and Liz is seated, leaning back onto us. We're all wearing mostly black, so we blend together, unclear where my torso ends and Leah's begins, or where Liz's shoulders meet our legs. I love this conjoinedness, but what strikes me most about this photograph, the thing that drove me to have it framed, is the look on all of our faces: We all look utterly serene. At peace, at ease, the relaxed countenances of three women who know they're in the company of people on whom they can safely lean their full weight.

Despite the shadow of a possibly irreparable fracture in my relationship with my mother, I tried to feel celebratory when my memoir was published. I made reservations at a nice restaurant for the evening of publication day, for dinner with Soomin and Leah—the two people I'd lived with while writing the book; two people who could be uncomplicatedly happy for me. We dressed up and drank champagne and toasted my accomplishment, and it felt, for a while, like a purely happy occasion. We didn't talk about my mother.

We did talk, though, about the ongoing indecision over whether Soomin and I would have kids. Leah was aware that "I just need to put this book out first" had been my primary deflection for the last couple of years, and now here was the book. We have the kind of relationship in which "So? Baby next?" was an acceptable question for her to ask, even though I'd probably kick a stranger in the shins for making a similar inquiry.

Leah had recently moved to the Upper West Side, where Soomin and I had lived for the last few years, and was loving it. "I think I might stay here, like, for good," she said at dinner that night. "So you know, if you do have a kid, Auntie Leah will be around."

I knew this wasn't an offer she would make unless she meant it. Soomin and Leah have the rapport of family, too—he understands and enjoys her role in our lives. When we got keys copied for our new apartment, he was the one who remembered to get a set made for Leah. That night at dinner, all of us giddy with the special occasion, clinking champagne flutes and taking lots of pictures, her comment could have floated past as part of a flowing conversation. But all three of us latched on to it as something important, something that could be a beginning.

We talked at length over our goat cheese salads and steaks about what it would really be like to raise kids in the city these days—how different it would be from when the three of us were growing up here, and what it would mean to have a friend a few blocks away who could take them to the park so I could write. For as long as I've known her, Leah has said with a conviction I envy that she doesn't want kids of her own, but we all agreed that night that she'd be the best cool aunt anyone could ask for. And the pieces of a future with a kid in it started to fit together in my mind more clearly than they ever had before.

At least one of my mother's two sisters was nearby for most of my childhood, as was her best friend, Hannah, my "fairy godmother." Hannah used to take me out for the afternoon when my parents needed a break, and sometimes overnight. When I was about four, she bought me a hideous frilly yellow taffeta dress my mother would never have agreed to, and I wore it every day until I grew out of it—a real-life princess dress. Years later, she took me shopping at Saks for my wedding shoes—a pair of metallic silver stilettos that cost more than my thrifted dress.

When I was a teenager, I occasionally looked after Hannah's kid, Vita. When I was fifteen and Vita was ten, picking them up from school twice a week and walking them to either drum lessons or soccer practice was the only reason I kept track of what day of the week it was. I spent most of my days lying in the grass in Tompkins with a forty, but on Tuesdays and Thursdays I stayed sober until after I'd safely delivered Vita to their destination. On the occasional evening that Hannah went out, I skipped a night roaming the streets with my friends to watch movies with Vita and their three-legged tabby cat named Freak—showing them *The Rocky Horror Picture Show* and *Purple Rain* and all the classics it felt important for them to know. We told everyone we were sisters, not blinking or offering any explanation as strangers' eyes went back and forth between my blond curls and Vita's giant afro.

When Vita was being bullied in fifth grade, I had them point the boy out to me one day at pickup, sauntered over to him in my combat boots and leather jacket, and said in a low voice, "Hey kid, just thought you should know Vita's got a big sister looking out for her. Watch yourself." He looked terrified, and Vita looked absolutely delighted when I turned around and winked. What I felt in that moment—the satisfaction of seeing on Vita's face that they knew they could count on me—that was mothering love.

The idea of best friends as sisters, and sisters as a kind of mother, and familial obligation to your friends and their children, was central to my upbringing. It's no wonder that Leah's offer made motherhood feel more possible—or that it felt so natural to step in and help Jael through the first year of teenage single motherhood. I was raised with the idea of mothering as communal, a job not exclusive to mothers.

After dinner, as we said our goodbyes on Broadway and squeezed into one more blurry selfie together under the street-lights, Leah threw her arms up and yelled, "Let's have a baby!" We all laughed, but I loved her so much for this promise that we would always be family. That if I do have a baby, I'll have someone to mother me through it, even if it's not my actual mother.

Liz was the first of my close friends to have a baby in adulthood—on purpose and with a committed partner. I half expected that holding my best friend's baby would make me want my own; that maybe I could follow her lead and feel less unsure. I even had a dream right after she gave birth that I was the one in labor, afraid, and she was there, reassuring me I was doing it right.

I was twenty-seven when Soomin and I got married, which felt, at the time, like the ideal age to have a baby. I knew my mother had been too young at twenty-two, and when you're in your twenties, thirty feels like the end of everything. So twenty-seven sounded just right, and more important, it felt right. Soomin and I were high on how in love we were with each other and with the future that was opening up endless in front of us. We were about to move from the impossibly tiny first apartment we shared into a much larger one, with a bed-room that could absolutely fit a crib. I felt, then, a craving I understood as hardwired, animal. I wanted to be pregnant in a visceral, urgent way. I wanted to feel life being formed inside my own body, to pour the love I felt for Soomin and for our life together into its own corporeal form that I could cradle in my arms and sing to softly in the cool blue predawn hours. I wanted to show a whole new person how to look at the world and see the magic in it, and to sit back and watch the man I love be gentle and playful with a baby that looked like him and also like me. I wanted all of this in a deep, bodily way. Knowing this desire was my biological programming, feeling its intensity in such a way that I could almost taste the hormones metallic on the back of my tongue, didn't lessen the pull.

Soomin wasn't ready, though. He was worried about practical things like finances and space and our work schedules. That all felt irrelevant next to the enormity of my desire for a baby, but I knew that pushing him into parenthood wouldn't go well for anyone involved, so I agreed to wait a couple of years, until we were both more settled in our careers. I pushed down that wild hunger and refocused on work, on building a more stable and established life into which to bring a new person, on finishing my book.

Over time, the hormones that had hijacked my brain receded. I felt it happening, like when the swirls and jolts of an acid trip slow and fade until straight lines are straight again and blank walls blank. With that animal hunger gone, the question of procreation became a rational one, and I haven't been able to come up with a rational reason to have a baby—only lots of reasons not to.

When Liz got pregnant, I thought being near her, seeing someone I love so much do this huge thing that I'd once wanted so badly, might trigger a new release of my own desire.

We went to the Frick together when she was eight months pregnant—round and magnificent. We walked, slowly, through the quiet museum, joking about the bored expressions of the wealthy women sitting for portraits. I snuck a photo of her standing, one hand on her belly, in front of a massive Jean-Honoré Fragonard painting (*The Pursuit*, from his series *The Progress of Love*—an aptly lush, bountiful image full of flowers and silk and movement). I was immediately scolded by a security guard, as I knew I would be, but I'd needed to capture this moment of my friend on the verge of motherhood, in the world while about to change it.

We had lunch after the museum, at the first restaurant we saw on Madison Avenue—a diner with red checkered vinyl tablecloths on the outside tables, in one of the thousands of outdoor-seating sheds that had popped up around the city that year, jutting into the street. Relaxed and satisfied with the day, we ate giant slices of gelatinous blueberry pie and talked about, among other things, the surreality of what was happening to her body and her life. I told her one thing about motherhood that scared me was the prospect of not getting to be alone again for years. "I love to be alone," I said, with a laugh laced with terror.

"Yeah," she said, sighing and tilting her head to the side, "but you kind of have a chance to get used to that ahead of time. I'm already never alone. She's always with me. She's here, right now."

We were both silent for a moment after she said that, aware of this other person present for what had felt like an intimate moment between the two of us.

I left that meal in awe, and so excited for Liz, but still not feeling the pull I'd once felt.

"Maybe once you hold the baby you'll feel it," Soomin said when I told him I hadn't felt the thing. I'd described to him in detail the hormonal high of baby-craving while I was in it, how carnal it felt, how consuming. And I'd told him when I noticed that I didn't feel it anymore, the two of us wondering if it would come back again someday, or if we'd eventually decide to have kids in a more pragmatic way. Me wondering privately if maybe that had been my window, and I'd missed it.

I took the train out to New Jersey to meet Liz's daughter when she was one week old, honored to be invited into this private, vulnerable space so early. I stared at her sleeping face, marveling at her existence, recognizing Liz's permanent pout in miniature. Everyone had been commenting since the first photo appeared on social media that the baby looks so much like her father, and she does, but she has Liz's mouth: beautiful and perpetually just a little bit indignant.

The baby's father placed her in my arms, where she fussed for just a couple of minutes before falling asleep. I held her for two hours while the three of us adults talked in quiet voices. I did feel a surge, but only of love for Liz, and for this baby—not of desire for my own. Whatever traces of baby-craving were left in my body felt sated by holding this tiny piece of someone I love so much, and I was reminded that the desire for a baby is often at least partly the desire to hold a small version of the person you love most, to mother them from the beginning. While that biological component is mostly associated with cis-hetero romantic relationships, here I was seeing its more expansive possibilities: to hold this small piece of a friend who has mothered me, and feel satisfied.

In my ideal conception of friendship, this would be enough. I'd be so present for Liz and her daughter that it would feel like mothering. But the distance between the Upper West Side and the Jersey suburbs is enough to make the closeness of running errands together, of stopping by spontaneously when one or the other has a bad day, of a quick glass of wine after the baby's asleep, feel impossible. I'm doing what I can from here, but the truth is that growing up has put some distance between us. Partly this literal physical distance, but also the distance of having lives that are mostly based in our respective homes, rather than the bar. Of having partners that are not each other. It's not because she had a baby; I won't blame motherhood. If anything, her pregnancy and the arrival of her daughter reminded me how much I want to be in Liz's life even when I'm not there physically. But still, I miss her in my everyday life now, like I used to miss her when she left in the morning after crashing at my place at the end of a late night out.

Leah and I live a few blocks from each other, so it's easier to maintain some day-to-day closeness, though of course not in the same way as when we lived together. We take walks together, and sit in the park and bitch about our actual mothers, and our aches and pains, and our careers, and build each other up to fight the world.

Late afternoon on the first real spring day of the year, we meet on Riverside. The sun is low enough that it doesn't hit any other streets, but it's slanted and golden here, all the way west, at the water. We sit on a bench facing the sun, closing our eyes to soak it in after a long winter, comfortable enough with each other that we don't say anything for the first several minutes; we just breathe and bask like house cats. Eventually we turn to each other, pulling our legs up onto the bench to sit on it the way we used to sit on our fire escape. Neither of us feels any pressure to look "put together" to see each other—this is part of how we manage to see each other often. It's understood that we'll probably be wearing leggings, and definitely no makeup, so it feels even more like we're somehow at home, even as a boat drifts by down the river and a group of tween boys run in circles, jumping back and forth over the low fence twenty feet from where we sit.

We talk about her crappy job and my recent hip surgery and her rent being raised again. After a while, I ask how she's so sure she doesn't want kids. She lists practical reasons—money and climate change—that I can't argue with. But I know those practical reasons aren't enough when they're competing with desire. I know because even though I agree wholeheartedly with everything she says and nod along, yes, yes, there's still a part of me that pushes to override that logic. Something that still feels inevitable about motherhood.

Then she says, "I remember thinking when I was really young, 'I never want anyone to feel about me the way I feel about my mother.'" And it feels like she's gotten to the truth—touched the fear that's bubbling underneath all of the rational reasons.

I sigh and nod, and we both look silently out over the Hudson, the sky turning pink now as the sun dips even lower. I imagine what it must be like for my mother, after how hard she struggled to raise me mostly on her own, trying to stretch a too-small paycheck to cover rent and food and bills and leave enough left over to buy something fun for me so I wouldn't know we were poor. She tried so hard. And after all of that, this gaping silence between us.

I don't worry that I'll repeat my mother's mistakes, though. I'm more worried that if I become a mother, I'll turn into my father. My father, who prioritized his art above all else and didn't come out of his studio until he was good and ready. Who was fully present when we spent time together, but left most of the day-to-day logistics of parenting to my mother. Of course, this was only accepted because he was a man. If I had a child but still prioritized my writing the way I do now, the way my father prioritized his art, I'd be seen as (and feel like) a selfish, heartless villain. There's no avoiding this wrenching split of identity, I know. No matter how fervently Soomin assures me that my career will always be a priority, there will still be a thousand small moments when I have to choose between my work and my child; and the work will only win on rare, precious occasions.

I have fond memories of waking up with Riley at the crack of dawn when she was four and five—when she and Jael didn't live with me anymore but I still took care of her sometimes—holding her hand as we walked to get pancakes and then to the playground, my body still asleep and my mind lurching toward consciousness as she told me all about her dreams and asked if we could go to the toy store later and said she had to pee again. Those days showed me that I'm capable, I have it in me to mother in that way. But they also showed me just how hard it is. Those days when Riley stayed with me, watching her was all I did. I was in college then, but I never tried to get homework done while she was there. Aside from the fact that I wanted to make the most of our time together, it would have been impossible. I remember that level of tiredness, the mental energy required to tend to a child nonstop, so that when they're finally asleep you can barely get yourself to bed. How, possibly, could I write under those conditions if I had a child now? I know people do it, but the way writer moms of young children talk about their experience makes it sound like torture—the bitterness with which they express a desire for just a few hours of uninterrupted time, the wistfulness and grief on their faces when they imagine where their careers might be by now if writing hadn't been shoved into the narrowest margins of their lives in favor of caretaking. It sounds like too great a compromise to make by choice.

I'm afraid I would never forgive a child for taking my office from me, with all of its loaded meaning. I explained this fear to Leah once, during another conversation in another park. Never one to sugarcoat, she replied, "Yeah . . . well, as someone with a mother whose career got sidelined when she had kids, they will definitely be able to tell if you feel that way."

I finally admit to Soomin directly that I'm not sure I ever want kids. That I want them less now than I ever have. That somehow, slowly, "not yet" has turned into "maybe not at all."

I try to express to him the dread I feel, the fear that motherhood is coming for me whether I want it or not. He doesn't quite get it—says he doesn't think that much about whether or not we'll have kids, only when we talk about it, and once in a while in passing. "I think about it all the time," I say, in the grave and slightly desperate tone I have used to tell doctors "It hurts all the time."

If we do it, he says, we'll be great at it, and we'll probably be happy we did it. But if we don't, we'll have each other, and travel, and disposable income. He says he'll be happy either way, and seems to genuinely mean it. This is both a relief and baffling.

When I try to examine the feeling of inevitability I have about motherhood, I sometimes think it's a biological urge that I need to be strong enough to defeat in order to live the life I want. But sometimes I wonder if maybe it's intuition, some deep bodily knowledge of what I actually, *truly* want, and it's the fear that must be overcome.

Liz asked me to promise, during that lunch after the Frick, that if I saw her disappearing into motherhood I would reach out and pull her back to herself. I held my hand up and swore that I would, grateful for the permission to butt in. Remembering this promise, I texted her a month after her daughter was born, saying that whenever she was ready, I wanted to take her out to a nice dinner, just the two of us, with wine and conversation about work and dreams and everything other than the baby. I wanted to remind her that the world was still there waiting, but didn't want to rush her since it was still so early. She responded, "What's your schedule like next week?"

We dressed up and went out and we talked a little about the baby, but also about what we were both writing, and the latest weird social media drama, and the old days. Since then, we've alternated visits, me (or me and Leah) going to Jersey to see her and the baby, and then Liz coming to the city for a grown-up evening.

It's on one of these nights without the baby that we sit on my couch and I ask Liz how she remembers those days at the bar and my old apartment. I ask her about motherhood, too, and how she was sure it was what she wanted.

"There's a lot of religious language around feeling called to do something," she says, "but I really did feel called to have a baby. And now it's my life's work to make her happy and make sure that she's not just safe, but thriving."

I tell her how grateful and impressed I've been that she

didn't even seem to have to reclaim herself after having her daughter—that from the outside, at least, it looks like she never lost herself at all. But how? I want to know. How has she held on to her selfhood and her time so securely?

"It is really a do-or-die situation," she says. "It's like, if I don't get some time to myself, if I don't get out of this house and just get away from her, I will hate her. So as much as I worried about it beforehand, it ended up not being an issue because I had no choice. It's just doing what you have to do to survive."

This is somewhat reassuring but also terrifying. I hear the urgency in her voice and recognize that even though it has looked so natural from the outside, she has been fighting for her survival these last few months.

She takes a sip of wine and continues, "And then eventually you get into your rhythm, and then you're not just surviving anymore, you're actually enjoying life and enjoying each other."

I start to feel hopeful at this point. We've finished the first bottle of wine and opened a second one, my cheeks are warm and it sounds so idyllic: motherhood and selfhood coexisting not in an uneasy standoff, but in harmony. I remember the ways I've heard some women describe motherhood making them more creative, more deeply engaged with the world around them, more alive. I imagine what I might see anew through the eyes of a baby, my baby.

But then Liz pivots and admits she misses her "old life," which she describes as very similar to mine now: living on her own time, working from home so she could keep her own hours and take naps and generally do what she wanted to do.

"I don't regret her," she says. "Her existence on earth is the most miraculous, precious gift. But maybe I wasn't thinking quite clearly about everything you really do have to sacrifice."

And then I'm back to fear.

I swing back and forth like this—hopeful to afraid and back again—on a daily, sometimes hourly, basis, despite trying not to obsess. I can't let go of the idea that this is a puzzle I can solve—that there's a right answer, and I can reason it out.

Sometimes I want to have a baby just to put an end to the anxiety of deciding whether to have a baby.

Maybe I'll have a baby by the time this book comes out. Maybe I will have decided once and for all not to. Maybe I'll still be spinning around in uncertainty. I don't know.

What I do know is that when I imagine what kind of mother I would be, it's the kind of friend I've been that allows me to see it clearly, and to believe I'd do it well. Whether I become a mother or not, it will always be my friends who have mothered me into someone who feels capable of mothering; my friends who continue to show me my own capacity for love, over and over again.

In the meantime, I'm writing this in my office—sitting at the vintage Danish teak desk I bought with part of my book advance, a splurge and a promise to myself. A shelf of books that inspire me is within arm's reach, a philodendron vine that I've nurtured from a cutting to an impressive monster crisscrossing the whole window and dripping down its sides. On the walls: my father's artwork, some favorite art postcards, and a framed family portrait of me and two of my closest friends.

Portraiture

A few months into our friendship, Courtney came over to my studio apartment in Astoria, and we dug through my clothes to pick a wardrobe for a photo shoot. She mostly knew me in the demure uniform of pencil skirts, vintage silk blouses, and cardigans that I wore to school, and I reveled in her surprise at how many past and alternate selves were cataloged in my closet: plaid miniskirt, black velvet gown, floral sundress, fish-net body suit, ripped jeans. After a lengthy deliberation, we selected a sparkly gold A-line minidress and red silk vintage pumps.

Once we'd picked the outfit, we wandered in the opposite direction from the train station, toward where the neighbor-hood thinned out, until we found the remnants of a construction site that looked like it had been there for a long time. Courtney pointed to a corroded block of concrete half as tall as me, and asked, "Do you think you could climb up there?"

As I climbed, in my pumps and party dress, she started shooting. The resulting image series is strange and a little comical—my pale arms and spindly fingers outstretched for balance, wind blowing the gold dress and my platinum blond hair in all directions. It ends with a satisfying shot—the vision executed—of me atop the concrete block, legs crossed, hair blowing back, staring down the camera. I'm not wearing any makeup at all, a direction from Courtney that I resisted. I tried to negotiate with her, *Just a little tinted lip gloss,* but she was insistent: a completely bare face to contrast with the exaggerated glamour of the outfit. Looking at the photos now, I notice the lack of makeup right away, think I could've used some lipstick and under-eye concealer, but I also see how it adds a vulnerability, an intimacy, and something unexpected to what could otherwise have been a rather typical shot of a glammed-up girl against a gritty background.

Through her lens, Courtney saw the sleek, stylish city chick that I hoped people saw when they looked at me—*and* she saw a softness and depth beneath that, that I sometimes needed reminding was there.

We met on the student newspaper, where I was an editor and Courtney was a photographer. She and Liz joined the paper together, and they sat along a back wall, talking over the Very Important Conversations I was trying to lead, along with the rest of the editors, until I shot them my "try me" glare.

I was a high school dropout on scholarship at a private university full of students whose parents paid not only their tuition but their rent, too. I bartended at night and came to class bleary-eyed and exhausted, but I did all of the reading and every single assignment and always raised my hand. I'd been out of school for almost four years, hadn't actually completed a class of any kind beyond an eighth-grade level before college. I vacillated between not wanting my classmates to know

I was any different from them, and wanting them to know I was tougher, worldlier, with more of a claim to this city they were traipsing around like they were the first young people to get drunk in New York. I felt worn down and tired while my classmates were shiny and new, and I resented them for it.

Courtney was tall with an athletic build, moving through a room like she was used to open space. She wore big chunky shoes and crop tops, her naturally blond hair in a swingy bob. She had a bubbly ease about her that I read as the result of too comfortable a life. One of her first pitches to the student paper was a series of photographs of students' shoes around campus, which felt silly compared to the self-serious reporting and editorials we mostly pitched to each other—but for the blogcentric media landscape of 2009, it also felt just offbeat enough to be a hit. Part of me wanted to dismiss the idea, but I also liked the weirdness of it. It was lighthearted in a way that I had forgotten how to access.

When Courtney started coming out for after-school drinks with the newspaper crew, it quickly became clear that there was more to her than I'd seen at first—her humor caught people off guard, unsure if they were the butt of a joke or in on the joke or if it was really a joke at all. She'd respond to their confusion with an inscrutable smile and an exaggerated eyebrow waggle. Then she'd pivot abruptly to earnestness, asking intimate questions, genuinely interested in what other people had to say—more so than the rest of us, who were usually volleying off of each other's wit, waiting for our turn to one-up the latest anecdote or quip. Then she'd try to get us to dance in the mostly empty dive bar. She was a wild card.

One night, Courtney and I ended up sitting at a bar just the two of us for the first time; she stopped deflecting with jokes and I stopped deflecting with bravado and we had a real conversation. Stools turned slightly toward each other, ignoring the bustling bar around us except when we looked up to catch the bartender's eye and gesture for refills, she told me about her parents' divorce, and growing up in a wealthy Connecticut suburb under extreme pressure to excel, compete, and conform to oppressively narrow, image-focused ideals that never quite suited her. As the night wore on, I realized that the version of her I'd judged so harshly had been a projection, a version of herself that she'd needed people to see when she was a teenager but was now trying to outgrow. It was a moment of realization for me, that people who seem so happy and together on the surface can have their shit too. It sounds ridiculous now, but I really did have to learn that. In the world I came from, people wore their damage like a mark of pride; I wasn't used to the idea that it could be under the surface, even while that was exactly where I was trying to shove mine—trying to project a different version of myself from the one I'd needed people to see when I was a teenager. We were both wobbling toward our adult selves, and for a moment we caught glimpses of them, sitting at a bar together, the armor of persona set aside.

Since the beginning, photo shoots have punctuated our friendship; one every few years, not scheduled or planned that way, but coming up organically when we happen to have the time or Courtney has a concept she wants to try. And in retrospect each one feels emblematic of an era of our lives:

That first shoot in Astoria when we were both finding our

footing as young adults, trying to stretch beyond the identities we'd embodied in adolescence. I can see the question on my face in the final shot from this series: "Am I doing it?"

Studio portraits she took in the offices of a magazine she worked at when we were both making our first real professional inroads after college—declaring our arrival. The lighting is exaggerated, stark; the shots tight-cropped on my face so you can see every freckle. A screaming charge ahead into the world.

Intimate group shots of me, Liz, and Carly when we were all living far apart in our late twenties, figuring out how to stay connected to each other as our lives expanded in opposite directions. We're all wearing silk, draped over each other languidly, leaning against the exposed brick of my bedroom wall. A moment of still and calm, of intimacy and steadiness, captured so that we could hold on to it. Courtney talked about the female gaze, and I felt the significance of the four of us doing this for ourselves and each other, not for any other imagined viewer.

I knew I wanted to write something about these images, and the experience of making them. The artist-subject dynamic had been on my mind—the responsibility that comes with depicting my loved ones, choosing which details about them to show to the world, turning them into characters to illustrate ideas that are creatively interesting to me. And so the fact that I have played the opposite role in modeling for Courtney throughout our friendship felt exciting to explore, the spark of an essay idea.

But it didn't feel like enough to just write about Courtney

taking photos of me. The photo shoots weren't as simple as us executing her vision; they were a collaboration. The electric current of artistic excitement, the feeling of a concept taking shape through conversation, riffing off each other's ideas—*that* was what I wanted to find a way to capture on the page.

So I asked Courtney if she would take a new portrait of me—if she would come into the process, and make something with me.

To start, I asked her to write down her idea for the portrait:

> The assignment, as I understood it, was to make a photo portrait of you—one that would be printed alongside an essay about our friendship. The image itself would offer its own representation of our dynamic, or at least reveal/refer to something about how I, your friend, perceive you. You were interested in a role reversal: you'd written portrayals of your other friends and now, in this essay, I'd be portraying you.
>
> Photography had played a recurring role in our friendship over the years, so this approach felt appropriate. In fact, you knew me as a photographer first, back in our college paper days—though I was only posturing then, aspiring to the glamour photography seemed to confer, angling for proximity to something metropolitan and cool.
>
> In time you became my muse. Tattooed and waif-like, with Courtney Love hair, big boobs, a nose ring, and one thousand ear piercings, you were the perfect aesthetic foil to the Connecticut WASP ideal I was raised with and in the process of exorcizing. You were witchy, faintly Victorian Gothic, with a mischievous

absinthe fairy slant. A look in your eyes like *Go fuck yourself.* I'd watch you roll a spliff with spidery dexterity, in awe of your long-ass fingernails, ladylike and lethal, and wonder what a spliff was, and how I could make you my friend.

Importantly, it seemed to me that you were already a fully formed adult. By the time we met in college, you had lived a whole life: lost a parent, dropped out of school, done drugs, moved across the country, moved back. What's more, you'd come so far that *those days* were now behind you. You'd reformed and adopted a new identity as our editor-in-chief, dressed with great seriousness like a character from *Mad Men*. On my first day of class, I thought you were the professor.

By night you worked as a bartender at a busy and beloved East Village dive—as if we needed more convincing of your badassery. There you'd serve me doubles in pint glasses, which you called "big girl drinks." You wore cut-up Harley-Davidson T-shirts before they were sold at Urban Outfitters and played pool and were good at it because of course you were. You kicked grown men out, *and they complied.* One night, some guy I'd been talking to eyed you from across the bar, cocked his head and commented on how hot you were, as if he was the first person to ever notice, like he'd discovered you. I wanted to laugh in his face.

So while we always had some other stated premise, I think that in truth, our photo sessions over the years were in large part about all of that. About us both being

> enamored with your unusual beauty, the personas you'd crafted: Lilly the Hot, Take-No-Shit Bartender. Lilly the Crust Punk Turned Editor-in-Chief. Lilly the Tarot Queen Mother Mystic. Lilly the Muse. And also about partaking in the fantasy of editorial photography. The roleplay of artist and model, working angles, capturing The Shot.
>
> Looking back, I can now see how performative it all was, though we committed to our roles in earnest. I see us aspiring, reaching for something beyond ourselves. My impulse for this project is to strip away all of that artifice to try to capture a portrait of the person underneath.

I'd asked Courtney for a description of her concept for a photo portrait; instead, she sent me a written portrait of who I was when we met. I felt a rush of emotion reading what she'd written—I felt loved, to be seen and remembered in such detail; and I felt a pang of longing remembering that girl I once was, the very act of remembering serving as a confirmation that those days are gone. I quit bartending years ago, to write and teach full time. Instead of wearing a push-up bra and red lipstick and making my living by being the life of the party, I work from home in sweatpants, with a cat on my lap. I stopped bleaching my hair platinum blond because I can't be bothered to wear enough makeup to offset it. I don't even drink alcohol anymore, sipping herbal tea in the evenings instead, before going to bed early. I love my quiet, calm life, but sometimes it's strange to remember how *visible* I used to be—all cleavage and attitude, staying out 'til dawn. Sometimes, for a moment,

I still feel like my badass twentysomething self. But most of the time, I know that the girl Courtney photographed in Astoria no longer exists, and sometimes I miss her.

I didn't realize until Courtney laid out her intention to forgo it how much a part of me craved the glamour of our old game of Photographer and Model; wanted to see if a glimpse of my old self could still be captured. So much of my experience of the world back then was about controlling how others saw me, modulating identities by the moment—the polished, ambitious student; the streetwise city chick; the brassy bartender. Being photographed had always been a way to see my many selves reflected back to me, to confirm what others did or did not see.

When I was fourteen, a photographer from *i-D* approached me in my godmother's vintage store on Ludlow Street, and ended up shooting a spread of photos of me for the magazine: sulking on my Lower East Side rooftop in a floral dress and unlaced combat boots; doing a ballet barre routine, pointe shoes and all, in my tiny tenement kitchen. Two years later, my friend Haley and I did a spread for *Purple* magazine, wearing heavy black eyeliner and bright red lipstick, looking skinny, sharp, and mean in designer clothes. I modeled for local designers and for photographer friends—in vintage slips and indie label dresses; on rooftops and in parks and perched on window ledges. Each time, telling the world how to see me—an elaborate dance to freeze in single frames the confidence, poise, and allure that I hoped to project all the time.

But Courtney had something different in mind for this shoot—not capturing a persona, but trying to see past it. The prospect scared me a little, but it also felt appropriate: It sounded like the project of friendship.

I went to San Francisco, where Courtney lives now, to take these photos. It was the last stop in a long trip that started with a work conference followed by a visit with family, and I felt frayed and depleted by the time I arrived. I'd never been to this apartment, but I walked in and set my bags down with the relief of coming home. As I bent down to say hello to the giant, handsome tuxedo cat who had come to the door, Courtney's partner, Hannah, started to warn, "Oh, he'll probably run awa—" stopping short in surprise as he rubbed his jowl on my hand.

I sat in their sunny living room, full of plants: hanging across the wide window, lined up on an antique ironing board behind the couch, and one large, heavy pot sitting on a skateboard. I admired the small, beautiful objects on every surface, delighted to find the back edge of the pink-tiled bathroom counter covered in evenly spaced pink rocks.

That night, Courtney and I stayed up after Hannah went to bed, sitting on the couch with the cats, and talked about the layers of intention behind the portrait—what I was aiming for in asking her to take a photo of me as the core of an essay, what she was interested in capturing. We circled around and through the concept of photography as an art form, and how her relationship to it was in the midst of an upheaval:

> I came to love photography for the ways that it forced me to engage with the world. But as time went on, I saw it start to come between me and my experience of life. I'd see something that moved me and my first impulse would be to snap a photo. I began to fear that by turning

meaningful moments into objects that could be introduced into an economy to be bought and sold, or posted to Instagram and traded for social currency, I was corrupting the things I cared about most.

By the time you approached me to take your portrait for this essay, I had put the camera down and was turning instead toward art that deprioritizes the object and centers direct experience. I was revisiting Marina Abramović and Yoko Ono, discovering Hamish Fulton and Tehching Hsieh, and looking for ways to create art in opposition to capitalist consumption. I knew you were hoping for another pretty picture. I wanted to say no.

But I was curious about the possibility of making something together that was rooted in a new set of values and priorities. I thought there must be a way to create a portrait that subverts objectification, that reaches for something beyond persona to get at some true thing between us. To remove the performance that happens when the camera comes out; remove the whole act of the "photo shoot."

And she explained the concept she had in mind to achieve this:

We'll sit across from one another for twenty minutes, maintaining eye contact. Using an intervalometer, I'll set up a camera to automatically take a photo every two minutes. I'll be present with you as your friend, just showing up as I am, observing you as you're observing me. I won't be playing photographer or making deci-

> sions about which moments of our shared experience are most photogenic. The photographs will be incidental, unplanned, unstaged.
>
> While we'll use photography to create artifacts of our communion, the focus of the thing will be on the communion itself, what may transpire between us. The immediate experience of presence between friends.

This was not what I had in mind.

What initially interested me here was the subjectivity of depiction—the impossibility of ever capturing the entirety of a person, in writing or photography; and how in the face of that impossibility, the choices that an artist makes when depicting someone close to them reveal as much about the relationship as they do about the person being depicted. How I see Courtney is not all of who she is; it's who she is in the context of our relationship. Who I am with her is a specific and unique version of myself that exists only in that context. Friendships as the tessellation of a person.

In writing about my friends, I had not been reaching for anything like objective representation—I had tried only to capture who each of them is *to me*. But I was also aware of what fun-house mirrors these depictions might be to them, seeing themselves reflected back through my very subjective lens. And so, an offering: I would allow myself to be exposed here, too—not in the way I am usually exposed in my own writing, where I divulge tender and vulnerable truths but am able to position and light them just so, to make them beautiful or to emphasize their ugliness for effect; but in the precarious way of letting someone else make decisions about how close to zoom in, what to reveal and what to conceal. When Courtney explained her concept, I worried that these incidental images would not give me the opportunity I had been looking for to play with the reversal of subjectivity.

But before I could open my mouth to express doubt, I realized that this discomfort, this loss of control, was exactly what I had asked for. This was the switch from artist to subject. Following Courtney's lead when she came up with something unexpected, something not quite what I had asked for, was the best—the only—way to make this a genuine collaboration rather than a project of mine for which Courtney provided a visual asset. It felt important that this concept genuinely reflected Courtney's current artistic interests—that she had taken the idea I'd presented and found a way to make it her own. Courtney is a true artist, always pushing into new, unexpected territory in her work across mediums, and this was a chance to capture that aspect of her creative self in the most genuine way—not by describing it, but by giving it space on the page, and letting it shape this creative endeavor we were embarking on together.

> LILLY: This feels kind of like you're calling my bluff. In my original conception of this collaboration, I asked you to create and curate the image, and that felt like giving up control. But also, you've taken photos of me many times, and they always come out flattering. So I realize now that there wasn't actually that much risk, even though it would have been your vision, your staging, your selection, et cetera. But now

it's like, well, I asked for it! These images will be not only out of my control, but out of yours as well, so who knows how they'll turn out. And I've committed to putting them in my book, even if I hate how I look. That's a real surrender of control.

COURTNEY: I feel like the whole exercise, beyond just the image, but what comes before that, may call both of our bluffs in a way. I think we're very candid with each other, and I feel like I'm myself with you, but I think there's also a deeper reality there. How much of any relationship is posturing or trying out a version of yourself? The durational eye contact exercise is intended to dismantle that and get at something that's wordless and based in feeling. Because I feel like love and friendship, if you're lucky, is rooted in that ineffable thing.

The next day, we walked along the beach—a perfect Northern California beach day where the cold ocean breeze requires jackets but the sun is bright and warm. Our boots crunching the recently wet sand, I bent down periodically to pick up a sand dollar. They were everywhere, littering the beach, but I was looking for a perfect one—not cracked or chipped—to keep. As we walked, we talked more about how photography can be used to portray a false perfection, and how its use on social media prioritizes documentation over experience. Collecting moments rather than living them. I found my perfect sand dollar, held it up in the sun, its smooth white surface unblemished, and then tossed it back onto the sand.

We walked through Golden Gate Park, perfumed with eucalyptus, and went to a bookstore across town to buy copies of books we'd urgently recommended to each other the previous night, to exchange as gifts. We stood at the counter to inscribe them, not feeling at all bashful about the earnestness.

Instead of going out to bars and staying out late like we used to, we ate small doses of weed gummies, which Courtney cut precisely in half on a cutting board. We clinked oversized wineglasses full of fancy probiotic soda we'd picked out at the grocery store, to go with the dinner we cooked together in her kitchen.

There was such ease and comfort between us, just being present, that Courtney's concept started to make more and more sense. What is that thing, that current in a relationship that holds you to each other, without pretense or projection? Could it be captured in a photograph?

I'd been so wrapped up in the concept that I nearly forgot to be nervous about the actual experience of holding eye contact with another person for twenty straight minutes—right up until we had everything set up: a bright light shining in my face, pillows for us both to lean on, and a camera right under Courtney's face, so it could capture as close as possible exactly what she saw, without obstructing my view of her.

Then Courtney started the timer, and we locked eyes. We both tried not to smile and then smiled and then tried not to laugh and then laughed, just a little, before composing ourselves. Then we both nodded almost imperceptibly, exhaling slowly, and started for real. It had been less than a minute, but how much less? During the first few rounds, I thought maybe I could keep internal time and anticipate the shutter click, but it surprised me every time. Each two-minute period felt like a different amount of time—the first few long, the next few shockingly quick, and then stretching out again as I lost count.

At first I was distractingly aware of my internal monologue, narrating what we were doing, wondering whether I was doing it right, instructing myself to stop narrating and just be present. After several minutes of telling myself *Okay just sit here and see what happens, focus on the moment, look at your friend—look, it's Courtney! Okay I'm looking at her, we're looking at each other, here we are, being present,* I decided that rather than trying futilely to stop the voice, I would direct it. I started talking to Courtney in my mind, searching her face for clues as to whether she could hear me. I decided to focus on one specific thing so I could ask her later if she'd received the message—something simple, something clear and easy to transmit. The color yellow, like sunshine. I focused on the color yellow, seeing different shades of it ripple across my mind, while also thinking the words *Yellow, the color yellow, bright like the sun, like sunflowers, the center of a daisy, bumblebees. Yellow, yellow, yellow. Do you see it? Yellow!*

By this point the intervalometer had taken two photos. Or was it three? We both startled at the first one, laughing again for just a second. We acknowledged the second click, two minutes later, with just the slightest changes in expression. And then not at all for the next seven.

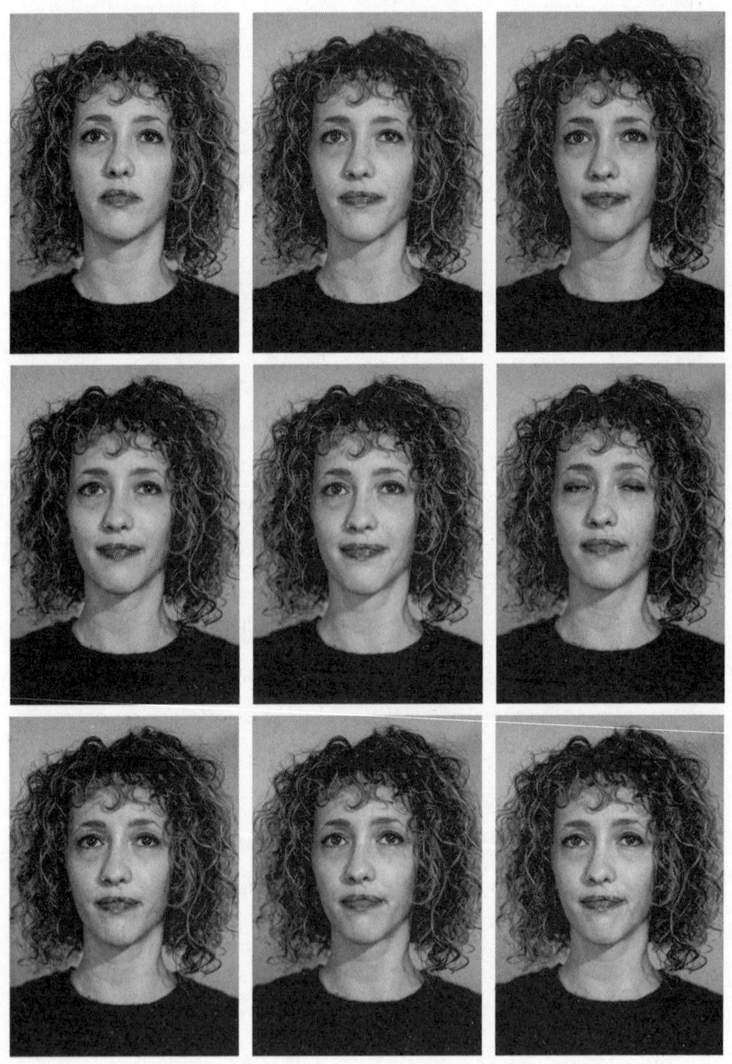

LILLY: I initially imagined that the nine images would look more varied. But then once we were sitting there, it almost felt like it would be cheating to try to communicate with you through facial expressions, and I wanted to see if we could get anything across to each other without even that. With just presence. But I could still feel my face moving in these really small ways, following what I was thinking and feeling.

COURTNEY: The variations in facial expression are so subtle, but when you look at the photos all in order it looks to me like kind of an opening of you.

LILLY: Yeah. In the beginning, I was very aware of being looked at, and the camera being there. And then as time went on, I tried to focus less on that and to just be present and open. Eventually I started having a conversation with you in my mind—about this project but also just about life and various important things we've talked about. And I wondered if you could hear me.

COURTNEY: Did you feel like I was hearing you? Or as you were beaming that out to me, did you feel anything back? Did you feel like there was a connection point?

LILLY: Yeah, I think so. But it's also not contextless, you know, it wasn't like we made a connection in that moment. It felt more like acknowledgment of a connection that was already between us. Like we were just sitting in that together.

COURTNEY: That's a good word for it, acknowledgment. There were moments I felt this feeling of like, "I'm with you. You're with me." Very simple.

It was only after the photo project, after the conversations about the concept and about photography in general and about the process of sitting for the photos, after I shared an early draft of this essay with Courtney, that we had an honest conversation about the ways the artist-subject dynamic had seeped into other areas of our relationship in the past. I'd been thinking of the subject as a position of surrender, while the artist is in control. But the subject is also the center of attention, with both parties focused on her and how she will be depicted and perceived. Early in our friendship, this was definitely the direction in which power and attention flowed between us most often, both when the camera was out and when it was not—the dynamic Courtney described in her written portrait, with her as an audience for my various performances of persona.

Over the years, we've made our way to a more even footing; to a relationship based on being present together, talking on the phone or in each other's living rooms about big life changes both external and internal. A mutual excitement and love free of posturing. That pure presence that Courtney tried to photograph.

But in asking Courtney to return to the artist-subject roles of our early friendship, I also opened a trapdoor for us to fall through together—one in which she stepped backward and I stayed in the limelight. I initially thought of this collaboration as a way to sit in the discomfort of giving up control, but ultimately I am still the one shaping our shared narrative. Sifting through our conversations, through her writing and mine, for meaning. This essay is about the two of us making something together, but the thing we're making is still a depiction of *me*.

But while the project calls back to our old, less balanced dynamic, it also feels like a true honoring of our current one: The best depiction of our relationship is not a story of past shared experiences, but an ever-evolving conversation about art and persona and what it means to connect. It's an energy passed back and forth, partially captured on the page but mostly intangible and mutable, soaring high and plunging deep at blink-or-you'll-miss-it speed.

And I'm reminded that in Courtney's conception of the project, it was always the act of sitting together that was the work of art—twenty long minutes of pushing ourselves not to shy away from each other's steady gaze, feeling discomfort, and awe, and love. She didn't see the color yellow, but we saw each other so clearly, and that experience was something we created together. The rest is just documentation—a sand dollar to bring home from a walk on the beach.

On Murder Memoirs

When I was deciding whether to attend the trial of the man who raped and murdered my cousin Sabina, I felt like I should go so that the jury would see me there. I knew how easy it would be for her to become an abstraction to them: *the victim, the deceased, the body*. To us—to me and my aunt and my mother and the rest of our family and her friends—she was still Sabina, still a real girl who we would never see or hug or dance with again. If we were all there, sitting on the bench behind the prosecutor, I thought, maybe the jury would be able to see that there was a real person missing. And maybe they would want to punish the man who had taken her from us.

I also thought I should go to the trial because I might want to write about it someday. I had already learned, at twenty-three, that the page is the safest place for me to try to make sense of things that feel senseless, too big to hold in my mind, too scary to say out loud. Telling myself I would write about what happened to Sabina *someday* meant I didn't have to fully face the horror of it just yet. I could put it on a shelf, where it would wait until I was ready to arrange it into something from which I could extract some kind of meaning. And whenever that day came, I figured, the trial would be an important part of the story I would tell.

But despite these two compelling reasons I felt I should get on a bus to Philadelphia and sit in that bright, formal room to hear the worst of human cruelty discussed in a discordantly procedural and orderly way, my body refused. Two years after her murder, my whole self was still clamped shut, bracing against the truth of what had happened to Sabina—to my first and favorite childhood playmate. The idea of sitting through detailed explanations of her final moments—seeing photos of her body in the dirt, hearing detectives and medical examiners describe the brutality enacted on her—was too much. I couldn't even look at the mugshot of her killer or read a single news article about what he had done, let alone be in the same room as him; hear his voice, see his body move through a room or shift in a seat, so very alive, while she was not. And so I did something that felt a little outrageous, if necessary: I prioritized my human self over my writer self. I didn't go. If I wanted to write about Sabina's murder someday, I would have to do without the firsthand courtroom scenes.

In the meantime, I kept working on the book I had started the year before Sabina was killed, a book about my father. I approached that story like a journalist—the job I was in graduate school to prepare for while the trial was happening—interviewing people who knew my father, trying to push beyond the limits of my own memories to put together something that felt more like a capital-T True story. Thinking like a reporter while writing about my father's heroin addiction, his art, his complicated and ill-fated relationship with my mother, and his death when I was twelve years old had provided something of a buffer between me and the ugliest parts of the story I was digging out of the earth like bones. I imagined that when I was ready to write about Sabina—someday—

I might approach the story of what happened to her in a similar way: I would read transcripts of the trial I hadn't been able to bring myself to attend; I would interview the friends Sabina had been with in the hours before she was killed, drinking champagne on a Philadelphia rooftop. I would re-create that final evening until it felt almost like I had been there, standing next to her while she laughed for the very last time. Someday, when I was ready, I would finally look directly at the truth of the way that night ended. And somehow, though I wasn't quite sure how yet, this would help me grieve.

When David Kushner's memoir *Alligator Candy* came out in 2016—six years after Sabina's murder, four years after the trial I didn't attend—it sounded like a potential model for the story I still wasn't ready to write. In *Alligator Candy*, Kushner, a reporter, revisits the disappearance and murder of his brother Jon when the two were kids in 1970s Florida, attempting to make sense of his life's defining tragedy using the tools of his trade. I thought it might help me start thinking about how to approach Sabina's story, while I waited for the emotional fortitude to shore itself up in me.

I got 94 pages in—to a scene where Kushner goes to the library to read the news reports about his brother's death for the first time—when I started to feel seasick, like the room was heaving up and down around me. This scene described something I still had not been able to do: allow the vague looming darkness to settle into the familiar shape of a news story. I squeezed my eyes shut, like I used to do on roller coasters before I finally admitted that I hate roller coasters and stopped going on them. I closed the book, noting matter-offactly that I wasn't ready to even read murder stories yet, let alone write one.

I continued to buy what I thought of as "murder memoirs" when they came out, which they did with increasing frequency over the next few years—a trend later identified as "true crime memoir," which felt at the time like a pointed reminder of what I couldn't yet face. I bought Carolyn Murnick's *The Hot One,* Sarah Perry's *After the Eclipse,* Rose Andersen's *The Heart and Other Monsters,* and Natasha Trethewey's *Memorial Drive* when they came out between 2017 and 2020, and placed them on my bookshelf next to *Alligator Candy,* unopened. I added older titles to my growing collection, too: Maggie Nelson's *The Red Parts,* Melanie Thernstrom's *The Dead Girl,* and Justin St. Germain's *Son of a Gun.* I didn't read those either.

I couldn't handle them yet, but I knew that eventually I would need to see how other writers had managed to write a "crime story" about something so personal and painful when, as far as I could tell from my previous associations with the genre—mostly the shows like *Forensic Files* and *Cold Case* that my mother devoured when I was a child—a good crime story required a certain degree of callousness, an ability to view cruelty with curiosity, even eagerness.

Portraying a real person on the page is always a subtle violence—reducing their multidimensional humanity, the unknowability of their inherent contradictions and mutable nature, into something flat and digestible. Even the best-rendered character on the page is only a fraction as complex as a real person. Doing this to a person who has been murdered—whose very literal humanity has already been stolen from them—feels like a larger injustice than doing it to someone who's still living and can flout your depiction with their continued humanness. Murder already threatens to eclipse a person—it is so shocking, so disturbing, that those of us who mourn someone who was murdered have to work to make sure the terror of their death doesn't take up more space in our memories than the living person they once were. It took me years to be able to feel anything other than horror and anguish when I thought of Sabina—to go first to her smile, her voice, her physical ease in a room, rather than to the way she died. But writing about a murder inevitably solidifies it as the defining detail of a victim's life.

So, I wondered, could I write about Sabina without reducing her to another dead girl in a story about male violence? Could I draw readers' eyes away from the brutality and toward Sabina singing and dancing down the street on a fall day with yellow and orange leaves wet and slick under her feet? Toward the scoliosis that made it look like she was always cocking her hip, about to say something sassy—and the fact that she usually was? Toward the way we used to take turns whipping cream by hand for the pies every Thanksgiving, sneaking taste after taste "to test the consistency," and how I used to always take one more taste after we'd settled down and gotten back to work, just to hear her laugh, and how she always did?

When Truman Capote first pitched a story about the 1959 murders of four members of the Clutter family—Herb and Bonnie, and their teenage children Nancy and Kenyon—to his editor at *The New Yorker,* he described a story about the impact the crime had on the small town of Holcomb, Kansas. About what such violence does to the people left behind. It was going to be about the victims, he said. Despite this stated aim, the resulting book, *In Cold Blood*, devotes more than twice as many pages to the depiction of the murderer, Perry Smith (and, to a lesser extent, his partner, Dick Hickock), as it does to anyone else. The Clutters are relatively thin characters, each reduced to an archetype: the hardworking father, the nervous mother, the popular daughter, the rambunctious son. The all-American family, a stock cast that could easily be swapped out for another. Meanwhile, Perry is given emotional depth, complexity, development.

Capote was not the first person to write about crime—not even the first person to write about it in an immersive, narrative style. But, as true crime expert Justin St. Germain puts it in his book *Truman Capote's* In Cold Blood, "Capote spiked a vein, and out came a stream of imitators, a whole bloody genre, one of the most popular forms of American nonfiction: true crime." And the genre he spawned has replicated his project's central contradiction over and over again: No matter how sincere the intention to center the victim, the killer is a black hole, pulling focus to himself. Murderers are enthralling in their aberration, and made even more alluring and terrifying by the glimpses of recognizable humanity that confirm they could be almost anyone. If we as a society are captivated by murder stories (which we undeniably are), it's no surprise that our fascination tends to focus on the most active and defining participant—the one who actually does the deed.

Many true crime books (and shows, and podcasts) are also devoted to the second most active character in a story of murder: the investigator. True crime as we know it today is the land of sleuths, both professional and amateur—from the older shows my mom used to watch on A&E to their modern heirs like *Making a Murder* and *The Jinx*, from books like *I'll Be Gone in the Dark* and *We Keep the Dead Close* to podcasts like *Serial* and *In the Dark*. Fans of the genre, having internalized the methods and perspectives of professional investigators, have begun taking on the role themselves, sometimes solving crimes that have stumped law enforcement (or that law enforcement couldn't be bothered to investigate with the vigor that police-valorizing true crime has advertised).

In sleuth-focused true crime, the detective or prosecutor becomes a stand-in for the reader or viewer as we try to understand how such a thing could have happened. They, more than the murderer, are our best chance at ever getting an answer to the maddening question of "why," because they're asking it, too. Their doggedness and cleverness and ultimate defeat of the killer are also the security blanket of true crime—assuring us that we are safe, that the monster will always meet his match in the end.

If *In Cold Blood* spawned the true crime genre as a whole, then *Helter Skelter*, the 1974 account of the Manson murders written by the prosecutor who handled the case, Vincent Bugliosi (with Curt Gentry), set it on the investigation-focused path it's largely stayed on since. *Helter Skelter* opens on the morning of August 9, 1969, when the bodies of Sharon Tate, Abigail Folger, Voytek Frykowski, Jay Sebring, and Steven Parent were discovered in the house on Cielo Drive that Tate shared with her husband, Roman Polanski—the audience enters the story at the moment it becomes an investigation. From there, the book follows a detailed timeline of police arriving at the scene; when each new clue was discovered, missed, misinterpreted, and finally put into context; and how the mystery was eventually solved and the killers brought to justice. Even the brief attempts to humanize the victims early in the narrative are couched in the perspective of the investigation, overshadowed by the crime. Brief passages about Tate, Folger, Frykowski, Sebring, and Parent—about them as living people with families and interests and plans for the future—are folded into the details of their autopsy reports, each one ending with the manner of death, presented in clinical terms. There's a self-awareness to this technique, an acknowledgment that once we've encountered them first as bloody corpses, it's impossible ever to see these people as fully alive; as anything other than murder victims.

The victim, in contrast to the fascinating murderer and dynamic investigator, tends to be the least interesting character in a murder story. She is passive; the main action of the story is something *done to her,* not something she does. And after her death, which is when the majority of the action in true crime stories takes place, she is offstage—only the looming specter of a snuffed-out smile—while the active characters play out the rest of the story. She is less a character, more an implicit threat: She could be you, or your daughter, or your cousin.

It is important to note, too, that the victim is representative of not just any woman, but almost always specifically a pretty young white woman. A Nancy Clutter or a Sharon Tate. The idea of the young white woman as a symbol of innocence under constant threat from vague and ever-present danger has been part of America's social fabric since frontier times and warnings of "Indian scalpers." White women's innocence has been an excuse for boundless brutality against Black men since slavery. It remains the easiest commodity to whip white audiences into a protective frenzy over. It is the bread and butter of true crime.

Sabina was mixed-race (white and Filipino), with brown skin, but she still got the Dead White Girl treatment from the Philadelphia media. Cynically, or realistically, I assume the public was so interested in her story at least in part because she had her white Irish American mother's last name; because it was her mother (my aunt) shown crying on the evening news. But also because the specific circumstance of her murder—a random attack by a stranger on a city street after dark—is one of America's favorite fears. Most female murder victims are killed by men they know, often their husbands or boyfriends. But a stranger killing is easier to imagine as imminent—lends itself better to dramatic music and goosebumps that might be the chill of the evening air or might be danger itself. In short: It's more titillating.

St. Germain posits that the shift in *In Cold Blood*'s focus happened because while Capote never met the Clutters, having arrived in Holcomb after their deaths, he interviewed Smith at length over the course of several years. And over the course of those interviews, Capote became fascinated with Smith, came to identify with him, maybe even fell in love with him. In one form or another, I think, the same thing happens to almost everyone who sets out to write true crime. These stories are always written after the fact, when the victim is already gone, making it impossible for a writer to portray her as anything other than a memory, a stand-in for the reader or the reader's daughter, a symbol of goodness. The killer or the investigator, however, is still there—still active in the story. Still a mystery to unravel, a source to interview. It's no wonder then that the murder victim is rarely successfully centered in true crime stories: Ultimately, no matter how fervently authors or producers proclaim otherwise, the story isn't really about her at all. Not, at least, when told from the perspective of someone who never knew her as anything other than a murder victim.

As I considered the inevitability of this trap, I became convinced that the murder memoirs on my shelves held the promise of the only exception—these were murder stories told by people who knew the victims as people first. Maybe, I thought, only someone who knew the victim could ever write a true crime story that didn't get sucked into the black hole of the killer, or fall back on the easy framework of the investigation. Maybe, when I was ready, these books would show me how to pull off the impossible: a murder story that doesn't further abuse the victim by reducing them to the violence of their death.

Sabina came to visit me in New York when she was twenty and I was twenty-one, and after a day of walking around the neighborhood, window-shopping and chatting and eating pizza, I suggested we get a drink. I knew she wasn't much of a drinker, but at that point in my life, every day was a countdown to when it would be late enough to go to a bar, and even though I'd been having so much fun with her all day, it felt like time.

"Lead the way!" she said with a smile—she'd been letting me play tour guide, up for whatever. We headed south toward Iggy's, the first bar I'd ever worked at, because a bartender who knew me would be there and wouldn't card. Iggy's is an Irish bar with a lot of the usual trappings—Guinness on tap, lots of dark wood, neon in the windows—but it's an Irish dive bar run by a bunch of downtown punks who love heavy metal and pirates, so the music tends to be loud, the bathrooms' filth a point of pride. Learning the ropes there at age seventeen was trial by fire, when the bartender I was learning from yelled "Tequila!" and handed me a shot every half hour or so while we kept the throngs of regulars and frat boys plied with Jäger. But it was a home bar—a block away from the apartment my mother and I lived in when we first came back to New York after a stint in California. She'd been a regular there for years; had reupholstered the leather barstools by hand; had persuaded her friends to hire her underage daughter when I needed work.

As Sabina and I walked into the dark bar, adjusting quickly from the brightness of the still-sunny day, we were greeted with hearty hellos from the bartender and a few regulars. I hooked my arm around Sabina's and, as we walked toward the bar, announced proudly, "This is my cousin!"

"Oh shit, no kidding!" The bartender dried his hands on the rag tucked into his belt loop and reached over to shake hers. She smiled sweetly and gave a formal "Nice to meet you" as he raised a bottle of Jameson and his eyebrows toward me, confirming that I wanted my usual. I nodded and he started pouring my double whiskey soda, asking Sabina, "What'll it be?"

She scanned the chalkboard of bottle beers, the rows of liquor, and the taps, before asking, "Do you have any champagne?"

The bartender let out a little laugh of surprise, and said they might have some somewhere. I smiled at her and shook my head—who orders champagne at a dive bar? It felt so perfectly her—undeniably and unapologetically sparklier than everyone else. Making a special occasion out of a regular afternoon.

She gave me a shy smile, explaining, "It's the only thing I really like to drink."

"Of course it is!" I responded, laughing and throwing my arm around her. "Only the best for Bina."

By then the bartender had fished an unopened, frosty bottle from way in the back of the fridge, laughing, "I think this is from New Year's."

"Fuck it," I said, "I'll take one too."

He poured us two wineglasses of champagne, setting mine next to my whiskey soda, and we clinked our glasses and said a cheers to each other and to the day.

That was the last time I saw her.

In a 2017 essay in *Slate*, culture columnist Laura Miller identified true crime memoir as a trend and highlighted a pitfall that's adjacent to, but slightly different from, the old problem with true crime in general: Rather than sidelining the murder victim in favor of a murderer or an investigator, Miller argues that true crime memoirists center *themselves* too much. I bristled when I first read this accusation four years after it was published—still doing cautious background research for a story I wasn't quite ready to write. It sounded to me like another version of the tired complaint that memoirists are self-absorbed navel gazers. At the same time, though, I felt a flash of a new apprehension: Would writing about my grief over her death make Sabina's murder all about me?

I have seen the way people cling to tragedies that are not really theirs: remembering a friendship as much closer than it was with a person who has died, soaking up sympathy like a thirsty houseplant. The cousin relationship is not as clear-cut as sisters or even best friends, and ever since Sabina's death I've struggled to articulate that we weren't the kind of cousins who barely knew each other and happened to end up in the same place during holidays; that I loved her deep in the pit of my being, and so her death cut that deep too. That I felt as strongly for her when she was alive as I do now that she's gone. So how to write about her death without the appearance of tragedy seeking? How to write about my grief for her without claiming it as primary, without overshadowing the grief of her mother, my aunt? I talked to my aunt Rachel about this concern and she waved it off, assuring me that my own grief is mine to express. But still.

Miller's essay complicated the ethical hierarchy I'd created in my mind, in which true crime memoirs ranked above true crime stories written by strangers—reporters swooping down like carrion birds to tell stories about people they never knew as anything other than "the victim." Now I was confronted with the possibility that a memoir about murder could be just as exploitative as any other true crime story. As I started to spin out, I realized that my hierarchies and suspicions and all of the plans and fears about what kind of story I might or might not write would remain theoretical as long as the murder memoirs I'd been collecting for years sat unread on my shelf. That I could ask these questions in the hypothetical forever, but would never figure out whether it was possible to tell a non-exploitative murder story until I took the leap and started reading and writing.

Eleven years after Sabina was killed, five years after my first attempt to read a murder memoir, I read Rose Andersen's *The Heart and Other Monsters*, about the death of her younger sister Sarah, which appears at first to be an accidental overdose but turns out to be—maybe—murder. Miller's qualms about true crime memoir struck a nerve for me, undeniably. But I swung back toward defiance while reading *The Heart and Other Monsters*. Yes, Andersen centers herself in the story, I thought; and why shouldn't she? The book is about what it was like to live with, and lose, her vibrant, troubled baby sister. It feels right that she be the one to write a record of her sister—her life and her death. And Sarah Andersen is so much more multidimensional on the page than any murder victim in a traditional true crime story. It is a story about *her*, not the man Rose suspects of killing her, not the cops that caught her case.

The book was hard to read. There were moments that called up unwanted mental images of Sabina's bruised body, and of her smiling face; poignant and painful articulations of the way that every happy memory of a person who was murdered becomes tainted, the shadow of the way they died at the edge of every image. I cried a few times, but I didn't get that seasick feeling and have to stop this time. So I picked up the next murder memoir on my shelf, and then the next, and then the next.

Sarah Perry was the same age when her mother was killed—twelve years old—as I was when my father died. The circumstances were very different—her mother was murdered while Sarah was in the next room; my father died in his sleep while I was on the other side of the country. But there are bits of the aftermath that Perry describes in her memoir *After the Eclipse*—the surreal feeling of being treated like a child when you know that the loss you've just experienced has abruptly ended your childhood; the feeling of being forever cut off from your middle school peers who have no idea how cruel the world can be; the rage of grief so powerful you scare yourself with it—that felt so familiar to me, the story got under my skin right away.

As I read on, I'm a little ashamed to admit, I also became invested in the mystery. The question of who killed Perry's mother looms large in the story, and isn't answered until nearly 250 pages in. I felt these two parts of myself—the grieving girl and the curious reader—in conflict as I read. I didn't want to be a voyeur, to be like everyone else, collecting clues and making my own guesses as to who might've done it. But also, Sarah Perry is a skilled writer who wove a compelling narrative. I understood, logically, that she knew what she was doing by not revealing the killer's identity until the point in the story when she learned it herself, twelve years after her mother's death. She wanted the reader to feel the infuriating empty space, the endless possibilities of danger. She wanted the reader to want to know. But even as I moved through the story in exactly the way I believe the author wanted me to, I also felt complicit. Maybe she wanted that, too.

In *Memorial Drive,* Natasha Trethewey's memoir about her mother, who was shot by her abusive ex-husband, Trethewey tells the reader right at the start that it took her almost thirty years to return to the house where her mother was killed. It took her that long to be able to face what happened. I felt a little bit of relief, then. Eleven years had felt like a long time to still barely be able to read stories about murder, let alone try to write the story of Sabina's. It was ten years after my father's death that I started writing about him; that felt like the inevitable amount of time. Like a deadline. But maybe it would take longer this time, and maybe that was okay.

I listened to *Memorial Drive* on audiobook, but had to

stop when I got to the chapter that consists mostly of a long transcript of a recorded telephone conversation between Trethewey's mother, Gwen, and her ex-husband, Joel. In the conversation, Joel explains over and over again, with a circular, detached logic, that he's offering Gwen a choice: take him back, or die. The audiobook is read by the author, and I couldn't stop thinking about what it must have felt like for Trethewey to not only hold those transcripts in her hands, but read them out loud—to read the words of the man who murdered her mother, telling her what he was about to do. My body felt cold, and I got a piercing headache. I paused the audiobook. I waited a week before coming back to the story, and when I did, I skipped the rest of the conversation transcripts until I was back, safely, in Trethewey's words—in her perspective, not the murderer's.

While reading Maggie Nelson's *The Red Parts,* about her aunt's murder and the trial, thirty-six years later, of the killer, I recognized glimmers of the type of scenes I might have written if I had forced myself to sit through the trial of Sabina's killer: Nelson describes the "little methods" she develops to be able to look at the autopsy photos, "Each time an image appears I look at it quickly, opening and closing my eyes like a shutter. Then I look a little longer, in increments, until my eyes can stay open." And the way her mother hunches over in her seat, "her chest hollowed out, her whole body becoming more and more of a husk."

I felt a twinge of creative regret reading these courtroom scenes—the memoirist's masochism, a perverse hunger for painful experience as good material. I had been right, I thought, that if I went to the trial, I certainly would have had something to write about. But mostly I felt grateful to my twenty-three-year-old self for knowing her limits—for recognizing a Rubicon and not forcing herself to cross it.

As I read these memoirs and half a dozen more, I was awed by the authors' ability to charge ahead into such dark and terrible woods. As I suspected they would be, they were able to avoid the classic true crime trap of sidelining the victims in favor of the more active characters because, unlike Capote and Bugliosi and every other writer or producer who has told a crime story centered on either the killer or the cops, they didn't enter the story after the victim was offstage. They were able to bring their loved ones to life on the page through their own memories; and to keep the focus on them, because their investment in the story was genuinely tied to the person they'd lost, not the intrigue or shock value of the crime.

But they also included the details that audiences have come to expect from crime stories. They read police and autopsy reports, painstakingly re-creating and describing their loved ones' terrified last moments; putting into words all of the unspeakable imaginings anyone close to a murder victim lives with, about what they must have thought, and felt, at the end. They walked into police stations and held in their hands articles of clothing stained with the blood of people they loved. They transformed the killers who had marred their lives forever into characters, with backstories and traumas of their own. In my awe, it was very clear to me that I was still not ready to do any of these things.

I still didn't feel physically capable of looking closely enough at the details of Sabina's murder to tell this kind of story about it—at least to tell it effectively, with the kind of brazenness of these writers, who don't let their readers slip into the comforting lull of the traditional true crime sleuth story. They prevent their loved ones from becoming passive dead girls in entertaining stories about killers and cops by keeping the horror, the too-real reality, brimming on the surface. They force themselves to look, and in turn they don't let their readers look away. I didn't have the fortitude to tell a story like that. And, I finally realized, I didn't want to.

I started to wonder whether there was a different kind of story I could tell instead.

If this were the kind of book I initially thought I would write someday, I would set out at some point to learn about Sabina's killer. I would go digging into his childhood, looking for what put such violence into him. I would wonder if a grain of hurt had settled deep in his heart, collecting layer upon layer of anger like a hideous pearl until it became too big to contain. I would pose the question of whether he hated women specifically, or was just a coward who liked his odds against a twenty-year-old girl better than against another man when the rage in him demanded a target.

But I don't want to know these things. I don't care about his childhood or what was going through his mind that June night when he first spotted Sabina and started following her, or during what came next. I don't ever need to know so much as what his voice sounds like. Don't need to let him become human for me; a character more defined than a fairy-tale wolf, a personification of evil. Nothing that could have happened in his life would make what he did make any sense, and the idea of searching for a reason feels too close to inviting sympathy for him—in myself or in a reader.

It is possible to write a true crime memoir without offering undue grace to the killer. In fact, most of the ones I read stand firm in their refusal to do so. *The Heart and Other Monsters* is divided into five parts, and the man who may have killed Andersen's sister is not given a name until part IV, referred to until then only as "the Man." He is part of Sarah Andersen's story, not the other way around. And Perry writes about her decision not to interview her mother's killer for *After the Eclipse:* "To be in conversation with someone, you must cooperate with them, however briefly, and I have no wish to cooperate with him." (I felt such immense relief reading that line—I had been bracing for such an interview since she brought up the possibility earlier in the story, and wanting desperately for her to spare herself.) But even these authors' demonstrations of how to keep the murderer out of the center of a murder story felt like more attention than I was willing to give. I don't even want to know enough about Sabina's killer to hate him with more precision than I already do. All I need to know about him is that he will be in prison until he dies.

It's been thirteen years now since Sabina's death, and I still can't bring myself to wade all the way into the horror of what happened to her. What's changed, though, is that I've stopped waiting to be able to, stopped anticipating that someday I will have to. I feel instead a self-protective impulse, a stubborn unwillingness to shine a bright light on the most horrible parts of this story.

In all of these murder memoirs I read, there was a sense that the writer felt it was their duty to look directly at the ugly truth. Several state this outright; in others it's present as an undercurrent, in the way the writers keep pushing forward despite nightmares, nausea, and visceral urges to flee. I felt this sense of duty when I was investigating my father's life, reading his journals and letters, sitting through tearful conversations with my mother and stilted ones with people who had betrayed and been betrayed by my father during the course of his heroin addiction. I had to keep going because I had convinced myself that if I looked at every detail, including the most painful ones, they would arrange themselves into a constellation of him. Maybe that's part of why I'm not driven to handle this story in the same way—I've already written an investigative memoir, wringing every detail I could out of letters, journals, and interviews, trying to conjure my father back to life. I've already reached the end of that road and found myself still alone, my father still dead. So I can't convince myself it would work if I tried again.

"I have spent years conjuring her body," Andersen writes of her sister, "have envisioned myself next to her as she died again and again." I understand this impulse. I have three dried seedpods from a tree in the lot where Sabina died, and sometimes I look at them and hope that in the last moments of her life, she was looking up at this tree, not at the face of a monster. That as she was fading into unconsciousness, she could no longer feel the pain in her body, or the fear—that maybe she felt even just a second of peace. I have looked at these seedpods and tried to transport myself into this final moment through them, to crouch in the dirt beside her and smooth her hair out of her face, wipe the tears from her cheeks, and whisper in her ear, *It's okay, you're okay, I'm so sorry. I love you.* But for whatever reason, the seedpods are enough for me to do this. I don't need the autopsy report, the trial transcripts, the sound of a killer's voice.

I spent years preparing myself to write a crime story, waiting for the desire to know more about Sabina's murder to bubble up in me. I expected it, but it hasn't arrived. When I finally sat down to write about Sabina, the story that came out was not about murder at all. It was a love story.

ACKNOWLEDGMENTS

Thank you, thank you, thank you to all of the incredible women in this book who I am lucky to call my friends. For letting me write about you, and us, and for filling my life with love. And to the friends I didn't write about: I love you too, I just ran out of time. I'm sorry!

Thank you to my husband, Soomin, for always being a safe place to land during the chaos, and for making sure I remember to live in the world sometimes, not just in my head.

And to my writers' group, Angela Chen, Deena ElGenaidi, Jeanna Kadlec, and Nina St. Pierre, who have been there every step of the way. I can't imagine my writing life without you all, and I hope I never have to.

Thank you to my brilliant and patient agent, Annie Hwang, who pushed me to focus and develop the concept for this book into something that had a chance. And my wonderful editor, Rose Fox, for seeing the vision, and helping me execute it, talking through every harebrained idea I had along the way. Thank you to Whitney Frick, Donna Cheng, Cara DuBois, Barbara Bachman, Michelle Jasmine, Corina Diez, and everyone else at The Dial Press and Penguin Random House, for turning it into a book and getting it into people's hands.

And to everyone who helped shape these essays, including but not limited to:

Terese Marie Mailhot and her cohort at the Tin House Winter Workshop; Alex Chee, Lacy M. Johnson, and their workshop group at the Sewanee Writers' Conference; Lidia Yuknavitch, Daniel Elder, and the Corporeal Writing BoBs; Krys Belc for your class on flash essays, which opened up the possibilities of the short form for me; Rae Pagliarulo and Alysia Li Ying Sawchyn for your helpful notes; Melissa Febos for your early feedback and encouragement; Jude Doyle, Jess Zimmerman, and Alisson Wood for your early endorsements; the Betsy Hotel, the Sewanee Writers' Conference, and the New York Foundation for the Arts for the residency and fellowships that provided time, space, and resources; Esther Bergdahl for your sharp fact-checking, and especially for saving me from getting a Sylvia Plath publication date wrong—the Plath Girls would have come for me for sure.

Thank you to Sari Botton and *Longreads* for publishing an early version of "It Comes in Waves," and Rachel Veroff and *Off Assignment* for publishing an early version of "In Search of Smoky Cafés."

WORKS CONSULTED

FIRST LOVE

Dillner, Luisa. "The Importance of First Love." *The Guardian,* August 7, 2009. theguardian.com/lifeandstyle/2009/aug/08/first-love.

Dixit, Jay. "Heartbreak and Home Runs: The Power of First Experiences." *Psychology Today,* January 1, 2010. psychologytoday.com/intl/articles/201001/heartbreak-and-home-runs-the-power-first-experiences?collection=100364.

Fisher, Helen. *Why We Love: The Nature and Chemistry of Romantic Love.* New York: Holt Paperbacks, 2005.

Grimm, Jacob, and Wilhelm Grimm. Translated by Ralph Manheim. *Grimms' Tales for Young and Old: The Complete Stories.* Albany, N.Y.: Anchor Books, 1983.

LaFata, Alexia. "We Never Forget Them: Are Our First Loves Really the Deepest?" *Elite Daily,* June 9, 2015. elitedaily.com/dating/are-first-loves-really-deepest/1055283.

PARTNER IN CRIME

Chen, Angela. *Ace: What Asexuality Reveals About Desire, Society, and the Meaning of Sex.* Boston: Beacon Press, 2020.

Darnton, John. "Author Faces Up to a Long, Dark Secret." *The New York Times,* February 14, 1995. nytimes.com/1995/02/14/arts/author-faces-up-to-a-long-dark-secret.html.

Faderman, Lillian. *Surpassing the Love of Men: Romantic Friendship &*

Love Between Women from the Renaissance to the Present. New York: Harper Paperbacks, 1998.

hooks, bell. *Communion: The Female Search for Love*. New York: William Morrow Paperbacks, 2002.

Jackson, Peter, director. *Heavenly Creatures*. Miramax, 1994.

IN SEARCH OF SMOKY CAFÉS

Nin, Anaïs. Edited by Gunther Stuhlmann. *The Diary of Anaïs Nin: Volume 1, 1931–1934*. New York: Mariner Books, 1969.

SAD GIRLS

Barron, Benjamin. "Richard Prince, Audrey Wollen, and the Sad Girl Theory." *i-D*, December 11, 2014. i-d.vice.com/en/article/nebn3d/richard-prince-audrey-wollen-and-the-sad-girl-theory.

Clark, Heather. *Red Comet: The Short Life and Blazing Art of Sylvia Plath*. New York: Vintage, 2020.

George-Warren, Holly. *Janis: Her Life and Music*. New York: Simon & Schuster, 2019.

Jahn, Mike. " 'Pearl,' Last Album Janis Joplin Made, May Be Her Finest." *The New York Times*, January 16, 1971. nytimes.com/1971/01/16/archives/-pearl-last-album-janis-joplin-made-may-be-her-finest.html.

Joplin, Janis. *Pearl*. Columbia Records, 1971.

Malcolm, Janet. *The Silent Woman: Sylvia Plath and Ted Hughes*. New York: Vintage, 1995.

Mlotek, Haley. "The Hidden Vulnerabilities of @SoSadToday." *The New Yorker*, March 24, 2016. newyorker.com/books/page-turner/the-hidden-vulnerabilities-of-sosadtoday.

Nickalls, Sammy. "#TalkingAboutIt: How We Can Use Social Media to Take Down Stigma." *To Write Love on Her Arms*, January 9, 2017. twloha.com/blog/talkingaboutit-how-we-can-use-social-media-to-take-down-stigma/.

Plath, Sylvia. *Ariel*. New York: Harper & Row, 1966.

———. *The Bell Jar*. New York: Harper & Row, 1971.

Tunnicliffe, Ava. "Artist Audrey Wollen on the Power of Sadness."

Nylon, July 20, 2015. nylon.com/articles/audrey-wollen-sad-girl-theory.

SPELL TO MEND A BROKEN HEART

Eliade, Mircea. *The Forge and the Crucible: The Origins and Structure of Alchemy.* University of Chicago Press, 1979.

———. *The Sacred and the Profane: The Nature of Religion.* San Diego, Calif.: Harcourt Brace Jovanovich, 1987.

Elliott, Jasmine, and Katie West, eds. *Becoming Dangerous: Witchy Femmes, Queer Conjurers, and Magical Rebels.* Newburyport, Mass.: Weiser Books, 2019.

Grossman, Pam. *Waking the Witch: Reflections on Women, Magic, and Power.* New York: Gallery Books, 2019.

Mickaharic, Draja. *A Century of Spells.* Newburyport, Mass.: Weiser Books, 2001.

Monteagut, Lorraine. *Brujas: The Magic and Power of Witches of Color.* Chicago Review Press, 2021.

Starhawk. *The Spiral Dance: A Rebirth of the Ancient Religion of the Goddess.* New York: Harper & Row, 1981.

Valiente, Doreen. *An ABC of Witchcraft: Past and Present.* Carlsbad, Calif.: Phoenix Publishing, Inc., 1989.

MUTUAL MOTHERING

Cusk, Rachel. *A Life's Work: On Becoming a Mother.* New York: Picador, 2021.

Erdrich, Louise. *The Blue Jay's Dance: A Memoir of Early Motherhood.* New York: Harper Perennial, 2010.

Galchen, Rivka. *Little Labors.* New York: New Directions, 2016.

Heti, Sheila. *Motherhood.* New York: Henry Holt, 2018.

Offill, Jenny. *Dept. of Speculation.* New York: Alfred A. Knopf, 2014.

ON MURDER MEMOIRS

Andersen, Rose. *The Heart and Other Monsters: A Memoir.* New York: Bloomsbury, 2020.

Bolin, Alice. *Dead Girls: Essays on Surviving an American Obsession.* New York: William Morrow Paperbacks, 2018.

Bugliosi, Vincent, with Curt Gentry. *Helter Skelter: The True Story of the Manson Murders.* New York: W. W. Norton, 1974.

Capote, Truman. *In Cold Blood.* New York: Vintage, 1966.

Gage, Sarah. "An Open Letter to Carolyn Murnick, Author of *The Hot One: A Memoir of Friendship, Sex, and Murder,* Which She Wrote About Our Mutual Dead Friend." *Medium,* September 22, 2017. medium.com/@whymisssarah/an-open-letter-to-carolyn-murnick-author-of-the-hot-one-a-memoir-of-friendship-sex-and-murder-5e5fef8f8c19.

Kushner, David. *Alligator Candy: A Memoir.* New York: Simon & Schuster, 2016.

Miller, Laura. "True Crime Gets Pretty." *Slate,* August 15, 2017. slate.com/culture/2017/08/the-true-crime-memoir-when-mfa-grads-and-literary-aspirants-write-true-crime.html.

Murnick, Carolyn. *The Hot One: A Memoir of Friendship, Sex, and Murder.* New York: Simon & Schuster, 2017.

Nelson, Maggie. *The Red Parts: Autobiography of a Trial.* New York: Free Press, 2007.

Perry, Sarah. *After the Eclipse: A Mother's Murder, a Daughter's Search.* Boston and New York: Houghton Mifflin Harcourt, 2017.

Schechter, Harold. *True Crime: An American Anthology.* New York: Library of America, 2008.

St. Germain, Justin. *Truman Capote's* In Cold Blood. New York: Ig Publishing, 2021.

Trethewey, Natasha. *Memorial Drive: A Daughter's Memoir.* New York: Ecco, 2021.

ABOUT THE AUTHOR

LILLY DANCYGER is the author of *Negative Space,* a reported and illustrated memoir selected by Carmen Maria Machado as a winner of the Santa Fe Writers Project Literary Awards, and the editor of *Burn It Down,* a critically acclaimed anthology of essays on women's anger. Her writing has been published by *Guernica, Literary Hub, The Rumpus, Longreads, The Washington Post, Playboy, Rolling Stone,* and other outlets. She lives in New York City and is a 2023 NYSCA/NYFA Artist Fellow in Nonfiction from the New York Foundation for the Arts.

lillydancyger.com

Instagram: @lillydancyger

lillydancyger.substack.com

ABOUT THE TYPE

This book was set in Fournier, a typeface named for Pierre-Simon Fournier (1712–68), the youngest son of a French printing family. He started out engraving woodblocks and large capitals, then moved on to fonts of type. In 1736 he began his own foundry and made several important contributions in the field of type design; he is said to have cut 147 alphabets of his own creation. Fournier is probably best remembered as the designer of St. Augustine Ordinaire, a face that served as the model for the Monotype Corporation's Fournier, which was released in 1925.